Tragic Theory
in the Critical Works
of Thomas Rymer,
John Dennis,
and John Dryden

Tragic Theory
in the Critical Works
of Thomas Rymer,
John Dennis,
and John Dryden

Joan C. Grace

Rutherford · Madison · Teaneck
Fairleigh Dickinson University Press
London: Associated University Presses

Associated University Presses, Inc.
Cranbury, New Jersey 08512

Associated University Presses
108 New Bond Street
London W1Y OQX, England

Library of Congress Cataloging in Publication Data

Grace, Joan C
  Tragic theory in the critical works of Thomas Rymer, John Dennis,
    and John Dryden.

  Bibliography: p.
  1. English drama (Tragedy)—History and criticism.
2. Rymer, Thomas, 1641-1713.   3. Dennis, John, 1657-
    1734.   4. Dryden, John, 1631-1700. I. Title.
PR633.G67   822'.4'01   73-2892
ISBN 0-8386-1312-8

Ce

PRINTED IN THE UNITED STATES OF AMERICA

Contents

Acknowledgments

I would like to thank the following members of the Columbia University Graduate Faculties:

P. Jeffrey Ford for making valuable editorial suggestions; Howard H. Schless for offering useful criticisms of my manuscript; and Joseph Mazzeo for counseling patience when I became impatient.

I would like to thank Don M. Wolfe, of Brooklyn College, for generously encouraging me to publish this work, and my brother William J. Grace for maintaining confidence in its completion. I also would like to express my appreciation of many gracious acts of human kindness on the part of my colleagues Theresa Halligan and Catherine Rita Martin.

I would also like to thank the following publishers for permission to quote from copyrighted material:

The Clarendon Press and Russell & Russell for permission to quote from *Essays of John Dryden*, edited by W. P. Ker. 2 vols.

7

Introduction

In an age of constant dramatic experiment, such as ours, to reexamine neoclassical criticism as it applies to tragic theory may be unusual. The fossilized image of such criticism as an embalmed and static set of standards congealed under the philosophical weight of Descartes, Hobbes, and Locke appears to have little relevancy today. It is true that this is the predominant form that impresses itself upon the whole, but considerable life and variety exist beneath the surface.

Thomas Rymer, John Dennis, and John Dryden have many ideas in common, but each reveals an individual style of mind. Rymer's is something like that of the technocrat who is delighted by systems and who seeks to find a computerized method of handling even the greatest complexities. If the data become too intricate, of course, the whole system threatens to collapse. Rymer, consequently, does not scrutinize the input too closely, but directs his energies to keeping the apparatus in motion. He subjects to method the tangled traffic of ideas in the Aristotelian tradition and finds that the results are merely a matter of common sense.

Dennis's style of mind is that of a conservative humanist who appears to be old-fashioned because he is more concerned with ideas than with appealing to his audience. His insights into the mental processes of the poet, into the need for novelty and movement in imagery, and into the genius's organic expression of passion and thought, therefore, remain unfortunately buried in the library stacks.

Dryden is a modern man with a decently hesistant mind—by necessity aware of what is going on. Although always seriously engaged with critical problems, he plays with ideas as skillfully as a master juggler who instinctively makes his act appealing and provocative.

All three critics consider themselves patriotic Englishmen and believers in progress. For Rymer progress in tragedy means a return to the method of the ancients; for Dennis, the reinvigoration by genius of what has proved sound in the past; for Dryden, the synthesizing, updating, and adapting of various traditions in the light of the needs of the present.

What use did these critics make of the Aristotelian and Horatian influences to which they were heirs? What were their attitudes toward Shakespeare? How did the prevalent values and conventions of their time affect their conceptions of tragedy? What ideas of theirs are particularly interesting now? These are the questions that this study investigates.

Tragic Theory
in the Critical Works
of Thomas Rymer,
John Dennis,
and John Dryden

1

The Context of Seventeenth- and Early Eighteenth-Century Tragic Theory: The Aristotelian Tradition

The critical principles underlying the theories of Thomas Rymer, John Dennis, and John Dryden are in each case derived to some degree from Aristotle's *Poetics*. However, it is important to realize that these critics' understanding of the *Poetics* was the product of *Cinquecento* attempts to conflate the *Poetics* with the traditional rhetorical criticism and that these attempts had been codified by seventeenth-century French critics. To recognize what is distinctive about the critical theories of Rymer, Dennis, and Dryden, it is necessary to return to the *Poetics* and to examine the basic ideas from which neoclassical criticism developed, for the purpose of seeing how Aristotle's ideas were transformed by the sixteenth-century Italian and seventeenth-century French critics.

The sections of the *Poetics* relating to tragedy that attracted most attention and that were variously interpreted most usually concerned Aristotle's definition of poetry as imitation, the insistence upon dramatic unity and probability, the comments on characterization, and the reference to catharsis.[1]

1. Citations from the *Poetics* are to Gerald F. Else, *Aristotle's Poetics: The Argument* (Cambridge, Mass.: Harvard University Press, 1957).

13

All critical theories, according to M. H. Abrams, consider four elements: the work, the artist, the subject matter (frequently referred to as "nature"), and the audience. Most theories, however, are oriented more toward one of these elements than to the rest. Aristotle's is primarily concerned with the subject matter or "nature."[2] According to Aristotle, art imitates not Plato's shadows and mirror images but the meaningful core of human life unencumbered by the accidents that obscure our vision as we engage in living. *Mimesis,* a process distinct from any other and relating only to the arts having an aesthetic end, supplies something different from what exists in nature or is produced by the utilitarian arts. *Mimesis* in relation to tragedy means the "making" of plots, the "making" of one action, a complete whole, not identical with any particular action in nature, history, or myth that it may resemble.

The genesis of art is associated by Aristotle with man's natural instinct for imitating and for enjoying works of imitation, even when what is imitated, if experienced or observed in real life, may be painful. Although the primary purpose of the tragic poet is to "make" one, complete, human action of a serious nature, he must also give attention to the effect of arousing in the audience the pleasure associated with pity and fear and to the internal demands of the work itself.

Some Renaissance critics' understanding of imitation, however, leads to the belief that significant models in ancient tragedy interpreted in the light of Aristotelian, Horatian, and Platonist commentary constitute the "nature" to be followed rather than human action, as Aristotle meant.

It should be noted that, although Aristotle recognized the educative value of imitation in general, he did not ascribe any intentionally didactic function to tragic *mimesis.* The representation of a

---

2. *The Mirror and the Lamp: Romantic Theory and the Critical Tradition* (New York: Oxford University Press, 1953), pp. 6, 10.

human action in tragedy, according to Aristotle, should bring about the pleasure associated with pity and fear—a pleasure related to the poet's skill in showing the causal relationship between the incidents in his tragedy. The catastrophe should involve people who have close ties to one another, and should somehow result from the hero's ignorance of this relationship. Aristotle implies that witnessing a tragedy heightens the individual's perception of the possible consequences of error. This perception and the resulting enlightenment effect an emotional purgation and encourage a keener response to reality. The experience may in the deepest sense, therefore, be morally, or humanly, beneficial, but such a result is achieved obliquely, and is not the first intention of the poet. His first consideration is the "making" of the work itself. Renaissance and seventeenth-century critics, failing to maintain Aristotle's distinction between the autonomous nature of *mimesis* and the persuasive nature of rhetoric, interpret the end of *mimesis* in terms of a more intentional, direct, and rationalistic conception of moral utility. For Aristotle, the imitation must reveal its own moral significance. For later critics, the poet must, in a sense, read his moral into his imitation.

In the seventeenth century, for example, the plot—at least in theory, if not always in practice—was regarded as a fictional means of amplifying a moral. Rymer is insistent that the poet must clearly make the plot serve the ends of moral and social utility. Dennis considers the plot the allegorical working out in a particular, unified action of a "fable," or fictionalized version of a universal truth, illustrating a generally applicable moral. Dryden, who eventually believes that character, manners, thought, and expression in tragedy are equally as important as plot, also regards tragedy as a means of moving the audience toward virtue, but his notion of how this purpose is achieved quite often reflects an aesthetic approach nearer to that of Aristotle.

In contrast to the later rhetorical interpretations, by plot Aristotle meant the initial "making" by the poet of a chain of dra-

matic incidents showing their effect upon character and the relation
of character in action to these incidents. Sophocles' *Oedipus*
illustrates Aristotle's meaning. As a result of the oracle's
prophecy that he will kill his father and marry his mother,
Oedipus chooses to leave Corinth and journey to Thebes. This
choice leads to the subsequent incidents in which he acts in such a
way as to bring about the very fate he sought to avoid. Plot, according to Aristotle, demonstrates choices acted out by the tragic
hero as he confronts the given circumstances of life and as he attempts by these choices to make his own destiny. The best
tragedy, Aristotle believed, presents a psychologically consistent
chain of cause and effect that ends disastrously (ix. 52al-10, p.
323; x. 52al2-20, p. 338). The catastrophe results from the in-
teraction of the outer world of given circumstances and the inner
world of the hero's mind and character.

Although Aristotle discourages depending on traditional
stories, nonetheless the poet still "makes" the plot, which comes
into being prior to the rest of the tragedy, even when he uses
already existing material, for mythic or historical events provide a
framework within which he can demonstrate the probable or possible causal relationship between character and action in relation
to circumstance. What Aristotle insists upon is the distinction
between the tragic poet, who is concerned with the creation of an
action or plot, and the recorder of mythic or historical events, who
happens to write in verse. Aristotle believed, for example, that in
tragedy the assigning of names to characters is subsequent to the
construction of the plot. After the character has been named, the
poet can introduce material that applies to the character specifically. A poet, therefore, should be primarily a maker of his plots
even more than of his verses; he should not merely develop a
traditional story with new verses. In other words, he must realize
that his primary responsibility—whether or not his material is
mythic, historical, or original—is to construct a plot showing
within the terms of his own creation a convincing relationship

between character and action and a plausible sequence of events in the tragedy.

Aristotle conceived tragedy to be the imitation of an action, written in language that has been made attractive by employing rhythm and song, using not narrative means but persons performing the action and completing, through the progress of events arousing pity and fear, the purgation of the emotions aroused by these painful or disastrous events. Tragedy, according to Aristotle, is the imitation of a single, unified action, serious, complete, probable, and characterized by a certain size, in which the central figure, who is virtuous but not flawless, consistent, and true to life, comes to disaster through some error or mistake. Although Aristotle did not consider the chorus an integral part of the plot, he believed that it makes an immediate appeal to the audience. Therefore, the dramatist should make sure that the choral songs in tragedy belong to his play and are not disconnected from it. He should use the chorus as Sophocles, rather than Euripides, did.

The ideal tragedy, according to Aristotle, must have unity of action. It must form a perfect, logical whole, with a beginning, a middle, and an end. Unity of plot, however, is not achieved by building episodes around one hero; unity requires a sequence of events following in necessary and probable order from the beginning to the end. Whether these events could follow one another in real life is irrelevant. Nothing should be lacking that ought to be included, and nothing included that does not logically belong where it is. Every part of the action must be essential to the whole.

Aristotle's reference to the fact that tragedy attempts to exist during "one circuit of the sun" caused violent debate among Renaissance scholars. It was the foundation of the Renaissance and neoclassical unity of time. Gerald F. Else, commentator on the *Poetics*, believes that Aristotle is describing the maximum stretch of time during which an impression of unity can be sustained by the audience. Aristotle, argues Else, intended tragedy to be of such a length that it can be experienced in a day, whether it be seen, heard, or read. Limitation or unity of time refers to the length of what can be experienced within a certain time span, and not to a period supposed to elapse within the play. According to Else, the length of the play indicates, first, the extent and unity of action. Second, the length of the play is intended to direct the audience's responses, since these responses differ according to certain differences in length.[3] Tragedy, therefore, in contrast to the epic, by necessity has a tendency to conform to a more or less uniform length. For this reason, Aristotle considered tragedy a more concentrated form than the epic in the means that it employs to achieve its effects. Aristotle makes no mention of the unity of place, although the presence of the chorus in Greek tragedy tended to encourage such unity because the chorus, which enters after the prologue, remains on the stage. The later unities of time and place, implicit in the works of previous Renaissance commentators, were distinctly established by Lodovico Castelvetro in his commentary on Aristotle's *Poetics*, first published in 1570 and in an emended and corrected edition in 1576.

The influence of Horace, whose *Ars poetica* was known earlier and better understood than Aristotle's *Poetics*, is partly responsible for Renaissance and seventeenth-century modifications of Aristotle's concept of *mimesis*.[4] Horace recognized the necessity for genius on the part of the poet, but he strongly recommended familiarity with the rules and skill in using figures of speech as tools to help the poet achieve a polished style. Horace also considered proficient imitation (not slavish copying) of classical models a useful means to mastery of the poetic art. Seventeenth-century French critics supported Horace's principle of emulation, but frequently regarded classical models as unchangeable pat-

---

3. Else, commentary on the *Poetics*, chap. v, pp. 215, 217.
4. For information on the formulation of Aristotelian - Horatian critical theory in the Italian Renaissance and the general rules for drama emerging in the criticism of Castelvetro, Scaliger, and Minturno, see Marvin T. Herrick, *The Fusion of Horatian and Aristotelian Literary Criticism, 1531 - 1555*. Illinois Studies in Language and Literature 32 (Urbana, Ill.: University of Illinois Press, 1946), pp. 1-117.

terns to be followed rather than as stimuli to the poet's own creation.

It is true that Aristotle, in saying that poetic expression should be clear without being ordinary, provided the basis for theories of stylistic decorum, but Horace is responsible in large measure for the tendency of later critics to regard tragedy as a form of rhetoric designed by means of pleasurable teaching to persuade the audience to follow virtue. Horace further defined the dramatic genre by saying that violent actions should not be presented on stage, that a play should be divided into five acts, and that only three actors at once should engage in dialogue on stage.[5]

Probability is another concept in the *Poetics* that undergoes changes during the Renaissance and seventeenth century. Since Aristotle believed that poetry is more philosophical than history, "the poet's job is not to tell what has happened but the kind of things that *can* happen, i.e., the kind of events that are possible according to probability or necessity" (ix. 51a36-38, p. 301). The difference between the historian and the poet is not that one writes in prose and the other in verse, but rather that "one tells what has happened, the other the kind of things that can happen" (ix. 51b1-5, p. 301). History deals with particulars; poetry with universals. *Universal* in this sense means speech and action on the part of a certain kind of person in accordance with probability and necessity, in contrast with the particular speech and action of a person recorded by history (ix. 51b8-10, pp. 301-2).

Probability in tragedy refers to what can convincingly happen within the work constructed by the poet, and differs from what actually happens or can happen in life as we live it. Necessity in tragedy means the heightened and selective representation of human actions in nature, history, or myth arranged in a consistent, credible, and meaningful sequence. It would be contrary to neces-

5. *Ars poetica*, ll. 189-92, *Opera*, with previous annotations by Edward C. Wickham and current annotations by H. W. Garrod (London: Oxford University Press, 1963; first published 1901).

sity and probability, for example, to present in tragedy an accidental or extraordinary outcome to a sequence of events. The *deus ex machina* device is contrary to necessity and probability in tragedy. Probability demands that, through the medium of language, potentialities subject to chance in nature be shaped into an internally consistent work of art. Probability and necessity, for Aristotle, refer to inner structure, to what is psychologically convincing. Aristotle does not have in mind the statistical average or the commonplace, but suggests that the poet depends upon a framework of creation that must be accepted by the audience. Aristotle further states: "One should on the one hand choose impossibilities that are (made) plausible in preference to possibilities that are (left) implausible, but on the other hand one's *plots* should not be made out of irrational incidents; preferably there should be nothing irrational about them, or if there is it should be outside the plot-structure." A sufficiently skillful poet, however, may risk "even a strong improbability" (xxiv. 60a25-35, p. 623). Ultimately it is the power of the poet's art, Aristotle suggests, that makes his unique work a convincing whole.

Seventeenth-century interpretations of probability tended to use the principle as a justification for attacking the fanciful and the romantic, as Rymer does. Dennis has a deeper understanding of Aristotelian probability, and Dryden treats the principle in relation to the complexities involved in the whole problem of imitation.

The seventeenth-century critical standard of decorum (meaning appropriateness of form, characterization, and style to subject matter) discussed by Rymer, Dennis, and Dryden may also be traced back to roots in the *Poetics*. For example, Aristotle indicates the lines to be followed in representing characters in tragedy. Characters who appear in tragedy, says Aristotle, must be morally good and clearly depicted, appropriate to their sex and temperament, lifelike, and consistent. An inconsistent character must be "consistently inconsistent" (xvi. 54a16-27, p. 455). The imitation of characters must demonstrate heightening and selectivity, yet render them lifelike and appealing. All characters, including invented ones, should resemble the nature of human beings in general. They must be probable: what a dramatic figure says or does must be the logical outcome of his character. The events in which he becomes involved must, in the same way, issue from character, and these events must also emerge from a convincing and credible causal chain.

The characteristics of the tragic hero, according to Aristotle, are directly related to the hero's ability to engage in tragic action and not to his value as a model of moral excellence, as is frequently the case in the seventeenth century. Such a person must be a fully human person of more than ordinary capacities, yet capable of making a mistake in regard to the specific experiences of his life. *Hamartia* implies missing the mark. Such an error reflects lack of skill but not lack of morality.[6] Moralizing critics have tried to make the flaw more of a moral weakness than Aristotle intended. "At its best, tragedy is a story of human blindness leading human effort to checkmate itself—a Tragedy of Error. The *hamartia* is the Tragic Error; the *peripeteia,* its fatal working to a result the opposite of that intended; the *anagnorisis,* the recognition of the truth."[7] Because, unknowingly, the hero has violated the laws of reality on specific occasions, he must suffer.

Aristotle said that tragedy deals with characters better than usual, comedy with those "worse," but his meaning did not pertain primarily to rank but to the totality of human qualities represented. His reference to the need for characters in tragedy to be good, appropriate, lifelike, and consistent was subsequently

---

6. William K. Wimsatt, Jr., and Cleanth Brooks. *Literary Criticism: A Short History* (New York: Knopf, 1957), p. 39.
7. F. L. Lucas, *Tragedy; Serious Drama in Relation to Aristotle's Poetics,* rev. and enl. ed. (London: Hogarth Press, 1957), p. 122.

interpreted by Horace in the light of passages in Aristotle's
Rhetoric—passages that analyzed types of characters according to
rhetorical principles—in such a way as to encourage the miscon-
ception in Renaissance and French formalist criticism that Aristotle in the *Poetics* had been recommending the representation of
rigid types and a tragic hero of high rank.[8] Aristotle did believe, of
course, that the hero must be a person of conspicuous prosperity
who makes a great error, but his emphasis was not so exclusively
on rank as that of Renaissance and French interpreters.

The doctrines of verisimilitude and decorum reflected in Italian
Renaissance and French formalist literary theory stem from
Aristotle's principle of probability and from his statement that art
imitates nature, but they are derived more specifically from
Horace than from Aristotle. In his remarks on decorum relating to
characterization, Horace insisted that the poet must make persons
represented in drama resemble those who exist in real life, if he is
to please his audience.[9] On the whole, Horace recommended
following traditional conceptions of historical or fictional characters. Achilles, for example, should resemble the Achilles of
Homer. "Invented" characters must be consistent and show an
overruling passion.[10] Their manners—the personal qualities and
characteristic behavior of figures in drama—must be appropriate
to their age, sex, temperament, rank, and occupation. Artistic
heightening of this sort establishes a decorum or propriety of
characterization according to type: the depiction of immediately
identifiable or flat characters who do not change or develop in the
course of the play.

Renaissance critics, on the whole, were concerned with the
representation of general rather than particular reality. The poet

---

8.   C. C. Green, *The Neo-classic Theory of Tragedy in England during the Eighteenth
Century* (Cambridge, Mass.: Harvard University Press, 1934), pp. 34-35.
9.   *Ars poetica*, ll. 153-78.
10.   *Ibid.*, ll. 119-24.

should emphasize the typical. This tendency, together with the Platonist concept of the universal as the ideal, the moralistic interpretation of *mimesis* as the imitation of what "should be," and the effect of rhetorical concern with teaching by example—by praise and blame—leads to the belief that the characters in tragedy, particularly the hero, should be models of exemplary behavior. Aristotle, however, is concerned not with the representation of flawless characters but with the depiction of characters convincingly drawn, even though the process entails making "consistently inconsistent" characters believable. Platonist and Stoic influences, along with the tradition of typical decorum inherited from Horace, reenforced by native influences such as that of the *Mirror for Magistrates,* therefore, contribute to the conviction in the Renaissance and seventeenth century that tragedy should represent idealized and stylized types. Thus, for example, Thomas Rymer would not permit kings in tragedy to be made accessories to crimes. Women must be modest, if not notably intelligent. Servants are not allowed to strike their masters, killing is tolerated only among those whose rank qualifies them according to the laws of the duel, and well-brought-up Venetian girls do not elope with Moors.

Aristotle's mention of catharsis is the part of his discussion of tragedy dealing with its effect upon the spectator. Two interpretations of catharsis that influenced Renaissance and later criticism are the homeopathic and the allopathic, both of which may be traced to medicine."[11] Homeopathy administered remedies that intensified the symptoms of a disease until, after a crisis, the body was restored to a healthy state by an evacuation of the morbid

---

11. For references on the question of catharsis, see Else, p. 225, n. 14. One of the most noteworthy medical interpretations is that of Jakob Bernays, *Grundzüge der verlorenen Abhandlung des Aristoteles über Wirkung der Tragödie* (Breslau, 1857). For allopathic meaning, see Baxter Hathaway, *The Age of Criticism: the Late Renaissance in Italy* (Ithaca, N.Y.: Cornell University Press, 1962), p. 210.

humors.[12] Allopathy was the method in medicine of counteracting a disease by applying remedies that produced effects different from those of the disease—purges for constipation, for example. By analogy to medicine, according to the homeopathic interpretation of catharsis, tragedy provokes a discharge of accumulating emotions, especially pity and fear, and thus restores the passions to health and balance. In connection with the homeopathic view of catharsis, reference is usually made to Aristotle's description in the *Politics* of orgiastic music as a cure for religious ecstasy.[13] Also by analogy to medicine, the allopathic interpretation of catharsis regards the arousing of pity and fear as a corrective to a lack of these feelings or to an exaggerated sense of well being.

A different kind of homeopathic emphasis is associated with the Mithridatic function of tragedy described, for example, by the Italian Renaissance critic, Francesco Robertello, who believed that tragedy administers a homeopathic remedy of pain by which we are toughened to the sharper suffering that life will inflict upon us.[14]

As a consequence of the rhetorical bias of later seventeenth-century tragic theory, consideration of the meaning of catharsis is mingled with explanations of the moral effect of tragedy. One explanation of the moral effect is the fabulist, which is based upon the separation of Horace's *utile et dulce* and the resulting division of a work into moral fable and sweet embellishment. Exponents of this theory regard embellishment as a means of teaching moral

---

12. Milton, paraphrasing Aristotle, in the Preface to *Samson Agonistes*, for example, speaks of the power of the tragic poet "by raising pity and fear, or terror, to purge the mind of those and such like passions, that is to temper and reduce them to just measure with a kind of delight, stirr'd up by reading or seeing those passions well imitated. Nor is Nature wanting in her own effects to make good his assertion: for so in Physic things of melancholic hue and quality are us'd against melancholy, sour against sour, salt to remove salt humors." *John Milton, Complete Poems and Major Prose*, ed. Merritt Y. Hughes (New York: Odyssey Press, 1957), p. 549. For Italian Renaissance critical interpretations of catharsis, see Hathaway, *The Age of Criticism*, pp. 205-300.
13. *Politics* in *The Basic Works of Aristotle*, ed. Richard McKeon (New York: Random House, 1941), Bk. viii, chap. vii,1342-2-12, p. 1315.
14. Hathaway, *The Age of Criticism*, p. 215.

virtue. The second explanation, the affective—derived from Aristotle and first put forward in English by Sir Philip Sidney —maintains that the emotions stirred by tragedy are in themselves avenues of moral energy because as a result of witnessing a tragedy we are moved to want to know and to want to follow what is good.[15]

Sidney's *Defence of Poesie* (published in 1595 under the title *An Apology for Poetrie,* and in 1598, in Sidneys collected works, under the title *Defence of Poesie)* argues that poetry teaches what is good and true more efficiently than history or philosophy because it moves man to act in accordance with what he has learned. The historian is limited to the particular events of the past, which may have no general significance, while the philosopher presents the universal in such a dull or difficult manner that he frightens the very audience that he seeks to reach. The poet, in contrast, provides "speaking pictures," images uniting the particular and the universal, which are easily assimilated by the memory and easily recalled when a man is confronted with real-life situations demanding a moral response. In contrasting the methodical teaching of the philosopher with the moving power of the poet, Sidney says:

> And that moving is of a higher degree than teaching, it may by this appear, that it is well nigh both the cause and effect of teaching. For who will be taught, if he be not moved with desire to be taught? And what so much good doth that teaching bring forth (I speak still of moral doctrine) as that it moveth one to do that which it doth teach.[16]

Ordinary men, in their own way, once reason has mastered passion, are capable of recognizing the value of virtuous action and of distinguishing between good and evil, for the words of the philosophers are only refinements of human wisdom. "But to be moved to do that which we know, or to be moved with desire to

---

15. Eric Rothstein, "English Tragic Theory in the Late Seventeenth Century," *ELH* 29 (September 1962): 307-8.
16. *A Defence of Poetry* [title given in Penshurst MS], ed. with intro. and notes by J. A. Van Dorsten (London: Oxford University Press, 1966), p. 39.

know, *hoc opus, hic labor est.*"[17] Sidney speaks specifically of tragedy,

> that openeth the greatest wounds, and showeth forth the ulcers that are covered with tissue; that maketh kings fear to be tyrants, and tyrants manifest their tyrannical humours: that, with stirring the affects of admiration and commiseration, teacheth the uncertainty of this world.[18]

Sidney considers the "affects" of tragedy to be "admiration," or wonder or awe, and "commiseration." Fear is reserved for the royal spectator. Sidney proceeds to refer to Plutarch's *Life of Pelopidas,* in which Plutarch describes Alexander, the tyrant of Pherae, weeping at the sufferings of Hecuba and Andromache as portrayed in Euripides' *Troades.* If the tyrant in this case did not, as a consequence of his response, reform his own behavior, the reason was, no doubt, Sidney suggests, that he hardened his will against the implications of what he had been moved by in the tragedy.[19]

In contrast to Sir Philip Sidney, Thomas Rymer, the most rigid expositor of the fabulist theory, analyzes the fable or plot of a tragedy in terms of whether or not it illustrates a significant moral lesson. The pleasurable effects of tragedy, according to Rymer, result from seeing the operation of poetic justice in the play.

Besides the fabulist and affective theories, another popular interpretation of the source of tragic pleasure was the aesthetic, which ascribed this effect of tragedy to the poet's skill. Two other explanations emerge about the middle of the seventeenth century. The first proceeds from Descartes, who held that the stirring of passion is itself a type of interior sensuality. According to Descartes's theory, the arousing of passion is in itself pleasurable, provided that it receives a check by reason. John Dennis expresses Descartes's view, although he was first under the influence of the

---

17. *Ibid.,*
18. *Ibid.,* p. 45.
19. *Ibid.*

fabulist André Dacier. Another interpretation of tragic pleasure proceeds from Hobbes, who maintained that the realization of the contrast between one's own comparative safety and the suffering of the tragic hero leads to a feeling of pleasure.[20]

English critics in the later seventeenth century relied particularly upon René Rapin's commentary on Aristotle, translated by Rymer in 1674. Rapin maintained that tragedy makes us capable of pity and fear; it also protects us from an excessive reaction to what is painful by accustoming us to the sight of human suffering. Our emotions are thus stimulated, yet at the same time brought into harmony with reason. This view modified the Aristotelian meaning of catharsis in the direction of moral fable, and the concept was made compatible with Christian morality, "not only by presenting a mildly securalized *caritas* as the proper result of the tragic emotion, but also by introducing a voluntarism which seems foreign to the *Poetics*."[21] Rapin, despite presenting an affective view of tragedy, tends to consider it a vehicle of moral rhetoric. Basing his views upon Cartesian principles, he held that pity and fear are the strongest and most disturbing emotions, and consequently the sources of the greatest pleasure.

In the second half of the sixteenth century, Francesco Robertello, Antonio Sebastiano Minturno, Julius Caesar Scaliger, and Lodovico Castelvetro are among the Italians who contributed to the mainstream moving toward French formalism by bequeathing to later critics fragmented versions of Aristotle's theory of imitation. Robertello made *mimesis* instrumental to moral utility. Scaliger identified with nature both what is made by the poet and what is imitated. To imitate Virgil was, for Scaliger, to imitate nature. The latter idea led to an emphasis on emulation. Castelvetro stressed credibility (action in conformity to the expectations of the audience but enlivened by the injection of the believably wonderful or marvelous); Minturno was concerned primarily with

20.   Earl Wasserman, "The Pleasures of Tragedy." *ELH* 14 (1947): 288-93.
21.   Rothstein, pp. 313-14.

rhetorical values.[22] Robertello, Minturno, and Scaliger, following Horace's recommendations in regard to decorum, developed a narrow propriety of type, and distinguished between tragedy and comedy on the basis of the rank of the characters to be depicted in each genre.

Attempts on the part of Italian Renaissance critics to interpret *mimesis* in the light of Horace culminated in even more complicated efforts to achieve verisimilitude in regard to ordinary or typical human beings while at the same time representing the Platonic ideal. An ambiguous concept of verisimilitude resulted. The central figure of heroic tragedy illustrates the desire on the part of later playwrights to represent in a single character normal, typical, and ideal humanity.

Verisimilitude as interpreted by the Italian critics shows at the same time a trend toward realism. Castelvetro, for instance, insisted upon looking to the tastes of an undiscriminating audience as a guide to what is to be represented in tragedy. Consequently, in the seventeenth century, the meaning of Aristotle's probability was further obscured by preoccupation with natural or factual probability, as it is, for example, in Rymer's critique of *Othello*, in which he points out how it is mathematically impossible for Desdemona to have had an opportunity to commit adultery with Cassio within the time span indicated at the beginning of the play.

One general effect of the Italian fusion of Aristotelian and Horatian tragic theory is that the dramatist comes to be looked upon neither as an inspired genius nor as an imitator of nature, but

---

22. Bernard A. Weinberg. *A History of Literary Criticism in the Italian Renaissance*, 2 vols. (Chicago: University of Chicago Press, 1961), 1:389ff; 2:747. Robertello's commentary on Aristotle's *Poetics* was published in 1548, the same year in which he published his Latin paraphrase of Horace's *Ars poetica*. Scaliger's *Poetices libri septem* (1561) shows his concern with tragedy as a means of moral teaching. See Bernard A. Weinberg, "Scaliger versus Aristotle on Poetics," *MP* 39 (May 1942: 339-40). Castelvetro's *Poetica d'Aristotle vulgarizzata et sposta* (1570) ignored moral utility and emphasized the necessity for an effect of credibility in tragedy. See Bernard A. Weinberg, "Castelvetro's Theory of Poetics," *Critics and Criticism*, ed. R. S. Crane (Chicago: University of Chicago Press, 1952), pp. 356 ff. On Minturno's *De poeta (1559)*, see Weinberg, *A History of Literary Criticism in the Italian Renaissance*, 2:737 ff.

as a follower of the rules and emulator of the ancients. There also develops a disparagement of fancy, of the marvelous, and of the unexpected in the interest of credibility. Aristotle's unity of action is frequently narrowed into the pseudo-Aristotelian unities of time and place.

As a result of a desire to create suspense in tragedy or to serve the end of moral utility, admiration, either in the sense of wonder or of veneration for great men, is introduced as a tragic emotion, particularly by Minturno.[23] Moral utility may sometimes also justify the representation of what is evil or painful in life. Finally, although the debate between the supporters of moral utility and the defenders of pleasure as the end of poetry remains, criticism of tragedy on the basis that it should teach morality becomes more usual than not.

Aristotle's critical method, based upon his philosophical consideration of tragedy as *mimesis*, infiltrated by Horace's more utilitarian recommendations and by a generally rhetorical emphasis, gradually becomes an un-Aristotelian system of abstract principles and rules, including that of poetic justice. Aristotle's approach to the work as a whole is frequently replaced by critical analysis of its parts. As a consequence, methodology and system are applied to the problem of how to write tragedy successfully. It is upon these critical confusions that the French formalists proceed to build a tight and organized theory.

Shortly after the death of François de Malherbe, beginning about 1637, with Jean Chapelain, Georges de Scudéry, and Jules de la Mesnardière, followed by L'Abbé d'Aubignac at the start of the second half of the century, and culminating in 1674 with Nicholas Boileau-Despréaux, the French formalists coordinated elements from the Italian critics of the sixteenth century. The ideas

---

23. For an explanation of the various and changing meanings of "admiration," implying at first "astonishment," associated with pity and fear—or awe—and later used in the modern sense, see J.E. Gillet, "A Note on the Tragic 'Admiration,'" *MLR* 13 (1918): 233-38.

of the earlier Italian critics were clarified and arranged by the less scholarly and less speculative French into a theory intended both to guide practicing writers and to serve as a standard by which to judge their work.

The system of French formalism related principally to poetry, including tragedy. It set up not only a core of general principles but a series of laws dictating the methods to be followed in composing various genres. The ultimate purpose of poetry was considered to be moral instruction. Although Horace's coupling of instruction with pleasure was not completely ignored, the main stress was didactic. It was also recognized that to be a poet requires a degree of natural talent, but little was said of the quality of genius. Poetic composition, it was thought, depended on a code of rules, submission to which was essential, and paramount importance was given to the poet's need to know the techniques of his art.

The rules also governed the various kinds of poetry. These rules were based not so much on the actual practice of great poets as on abstract conceptions resulting from analysis of earlier critical theories. Each genre was associated with an ideal structure representing its true nature and based upon its special subject matter, purpose, effects, and style. The epic was generally agreed to be the highest form of poetry.[24] René Rapin's *Réflexions sur la poëtique d'Aristote,* published in 1674 and translated in that year by Rymer, expressed the same general theory as Boileau's *L'Art poëtique* (1674), namely, that absolute and unchanging standards of excellence in literature, based upon reason and nature, exist and are attainable by following the rules of the ancients. Aristotle's rules are "but Nature methodized."[25]

Epic theory, systematized, for example, in René le Bossu's *Traité du poëme épique* (1675), extends its influence to dominate tragedy, binding it by the epic rule of teaching by example.

---

24. J. W. H. Atkins, *English Literary Criticism: 17th and 18th Centuries* (London: Methuen, 1951), p. 12.
25. See René Rapin, *Les Oeuvres,* 3 vols. (Amsterdam: Chez Pierre Mortier, 1695-1709), 2 (1709):126.

Aristotle's theory of pity and fear is either neglected or frequently interpreted in La Mesnardière's fashion to mean the fear aroused by the suffering of the wicked.[26] The neoclassical critics ignored the fact that, though Aristotle spoke of the epic, his primary interest was in dramatic poetry. Aristotle's basically aesthetic approach becomes transmuted into a moral and social one.

The rules of the French formalists narrow the conclusions of the Italian critics. The generally appropriate subject matter for tragedy is held to be historical, although Aristotle's distinction between history and poetry is maintained. Elevated thoughts and ornamental diction must characterize the expression; the tragic hero is to be of high rank. The five-act structure becomes standard, with only three or four actors appearing simultaneously on stage together.[27]

Formalism was not without opposition. Early attempts at a freer approach to literary questions were crushed by Chapelain and Scudéry, but questioning of rigid doctrine was kept alive by Pierre Corneille and Charles de Saint-Évremond, who protested against the tyranny of the rules. Later in 1674 Boileau's translation of Longinus prepared the way for a new critical terminology and method.

Formalism organized a clear and intelligible tragic theory, but in the process of rigid codification Aristotle's notion of imitation was distorted to mean copying ancient tragedy rather than representing the actions of men according to probability and necessity. Many of the characteristics of neoclassicism were misconceptions of Aristotelian theory. Aristotle's law of probability, for example, was frequently misinterpreted. Verisimilitude was looked upon as referring to subject matter; the superiority of "plausible impossibilities" over "implausible possibilities" and the permissibility of "consistently inconsistent" characters in tragedy were ignored. Although Aristotle was concerned with the unity of action alone,

---

26.   Trusten Wheeler Russell, *Voltaire, Dryden, & Heroic Tragedy* (New York: Columbia University Press, 1946), p. 13.
27.   Atkins, *English Literary Criticism*, pp. 13-14.

the unities of time and place were insisted upon. The French formalists also followed the Italian critics in considering the rank of characters the primary distinction between tragedy and comedy.[28]

Aristotle's method, in contrast with later adaptations of it, was inductive, historical, and psychological. Influenced by contemporary conditions in the fourth century *B.C.*, his theories rest upon an examination of Greek drama familiar to him with a view to establishing critical principles upon which to base a rational analysis of the nature of tragedy. Applying himself to the essentials of tragedy, Aristotle, in the area of judicial criticism, suggests methods that deal with aesthetic values. The ideal critic, for Aristotle, is not the expert or the specialist but the educated man who judges a work as a whole rather than as an assemblage of parts.[29] The dramatist's work, furthermore, "is not to be subjected to random comparisons; it is to be measured above all *structurally* against the pattern of events" that the dramatist chose or invented when he began to compose his work.[30] The shaping of the whole play is to be given primary consideration. It is the *Poetics* seen "through French spectacles," however, that forms the matrix of Rymer's tragic theory, and to a considerable extent that of Dennis and Dryden.[31] Shakespeare's innovative approach to tragedy provides a particular challenge to each of these critics, stimulating the expression of Rymer's combination of common-sense and formalist standards, Dennis's defense of genius, and Dryden's Socratic consideration of the elements from various dramatic traditions that might be used to form a new kind of tragedy appealing to the spirit of his own age.

---

28.   *Ibid.,* pp. 15-17.
29.   J. W. H. Atkins, *Literary Criticism in Antiquity; A Sketch of its Development,* 2 vols. (Gloucester, Mass.: P. Smith, 1961), 1: 76-79, 115-16.
30.   Else, commentary on *Poetics,* chap. xviii, p. 538.
31.   G.B. Dutton, "The French Formalists and Thomas Rymer," *PMLA* 29 (1914): 185.

2

Thomas Rymer's Theory of Tragedy: Common Sense and French Formalist Rules Applied to Shakespeare's *Othello*

Thomas Rymer's condemnation of Shakespeare's *Othello* in *A Short View of Tragedy* (1692) as "plainly none other, than a Bloody Farce, without salt or savour" has frequently been considered sufficient grounds to dismiss him as a critic.[1] However, T.S. Eliot, who in two footnotes remarked, "But Rymer makes out a very good case," and "I have never, by the way, seen a cogent refutation of Thomas Rymer's objections to *Othello*," was tempted to speak more highly of him than Dryden did.[2] Dryden, after receiving from Rymer a copy of his earlier work of criticism, *The Tragedies of the Last Age* (1677), wrote to Charles Sackville, Earl of Dorset, saying of the work, "'tis certainly very learned, & the best piece of Criticism in the English tongue." He noted Rymer's capacity for "finding out a poets blind sides," and suggested that no man would dare or could answer him.[3]

1. *The Critical Works of Thomas Rymer*, ed. with intro. and notes by Curt A. Zimansky (New Haven: Yale University Press, 1956), p. 164. Citations from Rymer in my text are to this edition.
2. *Selected Essays, 1917-1932* (New York: Harcourt, Brace and Co., 1932), pp. 97, 121.
3. *The Letters of John Dryden*, ed. Charles E. Ward (Durham, N.C.: Duke University Press, 1942), pp. 13-14.

Dryden was at first impressed by Rymer's arguments, but finally found them too narrow, too lacking in empathy, and too alien to an appreciation of Shakespeare.

After the publication of *A Short View of Tragedy*, Dryden, who had been indirectly attacked in the book, wrote to John Dennis, saying that English tragedy, despite its irregularities, far surpassed anything of the ancients. "Shakespear had a Genius for it; and we know, in spite of Mr. R———that Genius alone is a greater Virtue (if I may so call it) than all other Qualifications put together." Dryden acknowledged that almost all the faults Rymer found in Shakespeare were there, "yet who will read Mr. Rym— or not read Shakespear? For my own part I reverence Mr. Rym—s Learning, but I detest his Ill Nature and his Arrogance."[4]

Rymer is most interested, as was Aristotle, in the subject matter of tragedy and in the demands of the work itself. Although he follows the standard of common sense, he insists upon a coherent system of values by which to measure tragedy, and disparages the reliability of judgment based on popular audience reaction. Poets, he says, would become careless without critics to discern the flaws in their work. Rymer's interest revolves around the establishment and maintenance of the literary standards that he approves. Probably T.S. Eliot's praise of Rymer stemmed from the fact that he himself supported rational method rather than subjective, psychological response as a basis for criticism—or thought he did.

A common-sense approach is mixed with French formalist theory in Rymer's view of tragedy to such an extent that scholars disagree about which predominates. Common sense is related to what A.O. Lovejoy calls rationalistic anti-intellectualism, meaning a belief in the universal availability and verifiability of all that men need to know and the unimportance and questionable validity of all that calls for subtle and intricate reasoning.[5] Spingarn be-

---

4. *Ibid.*, pp. 71-72.
5. "The Parallel of Deism and Classicism," *Essays in the History of Ideas* (Baltimore: Johns Hopkins Press, 1948), p. 85.

lieved that Rymer's views are based upon common sense rather than upon formalist adherence to rule and precedent.[6] Saintsbury speaks of Rymer as having had a "charcoal-burner's faith in the 'rules.' "[7] G.B. Dutton opposes the evaluation of Rymer as basically a rationalistic critic, pointing out that Rymer consistently makes reason subordinate to the application of the rules.[8] F.D. Dollard holds that in *The Tragedies of the Last Age,* containing Rymer's earlier dramatic criticism, there is scarcely an idea not found in French formalist theory; he finds Rymer's later work, *A Short View of Tragedy,* more rationalistic.[9]

To understand the reasons for disagreement in scholarly assessments of Rymer, it is necessary to clarify what Rymer means by common sense and to see how common sense and Aristotelian theory converge in his evaluation of *Othello.* Applied one way, common sense depends upon a chain of reasoning by which conclusions are drawn from what appears to be readily apparent. Applied another way, common sense depends upon a chain of reasoning appealing from a set of established assumptions to what appears to be readily apparent. Common sense is prone to circular reasoning.

The standard of common sense became evident in England with *The Rehearsal* (1671), a play by George Villiers, the second Duke of Buckingham, among others, which attacked heroics from the standpoint of reason. Strictly speaking, the school of common sense in the neoclassical period wished to criticize art by the light of reason, without reference to accumulated rules or deductions from venerated models. Rymer's particular kind of uncommon common sense, however, tends to presuppose some

---

6. *Critical Essays of the Seventeenth Century,* 1908 ed., 3 vols. (Bloomington, Ind.: 1963), 1: lxix ff.
7. *A History of Criticism and Literary Taste in Europe,* 2nd ed., 3 vols. (Edinburgh and London: William Blackwood and Sons, 1911), 2: 392.
8. *PMLA* 29 (1914): 168.
9. "French Influence on Thomas Rymer's Dramatic Criticism," (Ph.D. diss., Univ. of California, 1953), p. 272.

familiarity with Aristotelian theory, although he denies that such knowledge is necessary. Poets would not imitate the ancients, he says in the Preface to his translation of Rapin's *Réflexions sur la poëtique d'Aristote,* were not the reasons as clear as mathematical demonstrations. We need only understand the principles, Rymer explains, to consent to them, because Aristotle established his theory not "of his own magisterial will, or dry deductions of his Metaphysicks: But the Poets were his Masters, and what was their practice, he reduced to principles" (pp. 2-3). Rymer regards the rules as the codification of common sense, or "Nature methodized." The opinions of Aristotle and the conclusions of common sense are demonstrably the same. Common sense enables us, says Rymer in *The Tragedies of the Last Age,* to recognize the superiority of the "reasonable" plots in ancient tragedy over the crude and illogical ones in English tragedy. "And certainly there is not requir'd much Learning, or that a man must be some *Aristotle,* and *Doctor* of *Subtilties,* to form a right judgment in this particular; common sense suffices" (p. 18). Even women rarely make mistakes in matters of this kind if they have the patience to use their heads.

Rymer does not identify common-sense reasoning with popular audience response. He calls critics who cite this sort of evidence "*Stage-quacks* and *Empericks* in Poetry, who have got a *Receit* to *please*" (p. 19). Dryden answers Rymer on this point in his *Heads of an Answer to Rymer* (1677) and in the Preface to *Troilus and Cressida* (1679) by referring to the reader's or spectator's psychology and by proving that the plays attacked by Rymer in *The Tragedies of the Last Age* have moved pity and fear in a high degree. Dryden also argues that the dramatist's purpose is to please his audience. Even though the plays of Shakespeare and Fletcher may be defective in plotting when compared with those of the ancients, states Dryden, the means employed by the English dramatists have proved successful from the viewpoint of the audience. They "have written to the genius of the age and nation in which they lived." Nature and reason may be the same in all places, as Rymer claims, "yet the climate, the age, the disposition of the people, to whom a poet writes, may be so different, that what pleased the Greeks would not satisfy an English audience."[10]

Rymer's common-sense approach accords with the attempts of Thomas Hobbes and John Locke to discover operations of the mind as regular as the laws of mathematics. Since human nature, according to Rymer, is universally the same in every age, beneath surface divergencies of language, dress, and social institutions, it follows that under favorable conditions all men are able to arrive at the same conclusions. What is true must be comprehensible by the majority. Rymer assumed that a certain element of intelligence was equal in all men, although, of course, they might use this reasoning power differently, or passion or fancy might intervene to prevent their reaching the same conclusions. Those who use their reasoning power correctly, however, must eventually agree. Common sense, therefore, implies for Rymer the reasoning of the enlightened man who can follow a logical sequence of thought resulting from his own experience and accept the judgments of competent authorities, in contrast to the complex, or even eccentric, reasoning of the more subjective thinker. Rymer's common-sense viewpoint as a result is characterized by limitations that arise from its basic resistance to imaginative and irrational dimensions of experience. Rymer's common sense in this respect may be associated with the Cartesian insistence upon the supremacy of reason—especially when used as an abstract instrument, unobstructed by custom and prejudice—and upon the uniformity of natural law. Descartes also influenced a trend to look not to the

---

10. *Heads of an Answer to Rymer*, in *The Works of John Dryden*, ed. Walter Scott and George Saintsbury, 18 vols. (Edinburgh: W. Paterson, 1882-1893), 15 (1892): 385.

ancients but to nature: "Nature herself, as the Great Machine, hardly needed any methodising to yield the 'rules' of art."[11] Rymer reconciles a similar tendency in common-sense reasoning with his veneration of the ancients by assuming that when men examine nature reasonably they will come to the same conclusions reached by the ancients, who have established for all time a universal set of clear and orderly principles.

In criticism, Rymer believes, the discovery of dramatic principles begins with common sense. One of the first acts of reason is to imitate nature. Since the conclusions of common sense ultimately correspond with the standards of the ancients, to imitate the Greeks is a way of imitating nature. Prior to the seventeenth century when a historical approach to criticism began to develop, writers of ancient Greece and Rome were usually viewed as not very distant from contemporary English writers.[12] In his comparison of ancient, classical tragedy with Elizabethan tragedy, for example, Rymer is unhistorical, repudiating, as he does, the value of a distinctly English dramatic tradition in favor of the Greek. In *The Tragedies of the Last Age,* he states that the philosophy of the ancients is not so different from that of his own time, but the English "have forc'd another way to the *wood*: a *by-road,* that runs directly cross to that of *Nature, Manners,* and *Philosophy* which gain'd the *Ancients* so great veneration" (p. 18). If the English dramatists had avoided taking a wrong turn and had started with the foundations of tragedy established by Sophocles and Euripides, or had imitated "their *model,*" English drama would have outshone the best of Greece and Rome. Rymer would not admit, as Dryden did, that a new age might require a new kind of tragedy. To those who may object that there is a difference between drama that is satisfactory to London and to an-

---

11. Basil Willey, *The Seventeenth Century Background* (London: Chatto & Windus, 1942), p. 90.
12. René Wellek, *The Rise of English Literary History* (Chapel Hill, N.C.: University of North Carolina Press, 1941), p. 26.

cient Athens, Rymer replies that man and nature are always the same everywhere. "What mov'd *pity* there, will *here* also produce the same effect" (p. 19). By the time Rymer writes *A Short View of Tragedy,* his position has become so extreme that he insists that the method of English drama be abandoned in favor of a return to the model of Aeschylus. For Rymer, the whole question ultimately reduces itself to the fact that since Greek tragedy excels the English, it is only common sense for the English to imitate the Greeks. Rymer was not a confirmed ancient, however, except in his belief in the superior achievement of the Greeks in tragedy. His faith in reason and progress places him among the moderns. In his Preface to Rapin, he had asserted his confidence in the potentialities of the English language and in the promise of English literary genius. Although the English have not distinguished themselves in epic poetry, "for the *Drama,* the World has nothing to be compared with us," said Rymer, most probably commenting on heroic tragedy (p.10). He never repudiated his faith in modern literature, but his later pronouncements on tragedy were so strongly based upon his admiration of the Greeks that he came to be considered a staunch supporter of the ancients against the moderns.

Although it has been noted that such scholars as Spingarn, Saintsbury, Dutton, and Dollard differ about the extent to which Rymer expresses a common-sense approach to criticism, they concur in regarding Rymer as one of the transmitters into England of French formalist theory. Nevertheless, because his psychology in applying French theory is rationalistic, common sense can be considered an implicit standard affecting Rymer's judgments. For him, there is no conflict between the conclusions of common sense and the standards of French neoclassicism. They are the same.

At the close of the sixteenth century the rules of Aristotle as formulated by the Italians dominated European literary criticism. The first English reflections of Aristotle's theories, found, for example, in Sir Philip Sidney's *Defence of Poesie* and in Ben

Jonson's *Discoveries* or *Timber,* were mixed with Horatian maxims and continental scholarship. The influence of the Italian critics was first paramount, followed by that of the Dutchman Daniel Heinsius, and finally of the French, whose theories eventually became most influential. Rymer's *Tragedies of the Last Age, Considered and Examined by the Practice of the Ancients, and by the Common Sense of All Ages* reflects French interpretations of Aristotle, although Rymer was also familiar with Italian critical theory and with the work of Heinsius, the leading Dutch scholar of the *Poetics*, whose study was published in 1611. Taking from the French the Aristotelian examination of a play in terms of plot, character, thought, and expression, Rymer establishes this method as a common practice in English criticism.[13]

In addition to setting forth his critical method in the introduction to *The Tragedies of the Last Age,* Rymer also makes these points in answer to possible objections to his method: (1) Mere audience response cannot be a reliable test of drama, because only a reasonable judgment of a tragedy is valid. Particular audience reaction may merely reflect the ignorance of the group; (2) A comparison between ancient and modern drama is justified because man and nature do not change; (3) Reason and poetry are not incompatible because reason must always control the excesses of fancy; (4) The rules do not inhibit invention, restrain "good intrigue," or make all plays alike. On the contrary, they permit the representation of varieties of beauty while at the same time excluding the imitation of "deform'd" nature (pp. 19-20).

Using the form of a letter to Sir Fleetwood Sheppard, Rymer speaks of examining *Rollo, A King and No King,* and *The Maid's Tragedy* by Beaumont and Fletcher, *Othello* and *Julius Caesar* by Shakespeare, and *Catiline* by Ben Jonson.[14] Actually, he discus-

13.   Marvin T. Herrick, *The Poetics of Aristotle in England* (New Haven: Yale University Press, 1930), pp. 24, 36-38, 57.
14.   Curt A. Zimansky notes that Sir Fleetwood Sheppard was a fellow member with Rymer at Gray's Inn. As a companion of Charles Sedley and John Wilmot, Earl of Rochester, and friend of Charles Sackville, Sixth Earl of Dorset, Sheppard may have introduced Rymer to London's literary world (Rymer, *Critical Works,* p. xiii).

ses only the plays by Beaumont and Fletcher—and briefly *Catiline*—not treating those by Shakespeare until *A Short View of Tragedy*. In dealing with Beaumont and Fletcher's plays, Rymer first summarizes the plot of the play to be investigated, and then examines the play according to the Aristotelian divisions of plot, character, thought, and expression, following fairly closely the sequence of the play's text. Third, he uses the method of comparative criticism by referring to contrasting treatments of similar themes in Greek tragedy or by drawing attention to an abstract theory of what tragedy ought to be. Fourth, he frequently makes suggestions for revisions of the play being discussed to show how, by judicious imitation of the Greeks, English tragedy may be brought to approach or surpass the excellence of ancient tragedy. Fifth, he judges the play according to the standards of common sense, conformity to nature (in *The Tragedies of the Last Age* most usually considered as the ideal), and the rules of the French formalists in general.

Rymer differs from the French formalists, however, in emphasizing common sense and in making pleasure the chief end of poetry. The French more often considered its primary purpose to be instruction. Rymer adds that tragedy cannot please without profiting, although, he states, some poetry can please without being morally beneficial. The French critics frequently add that poetry cannot profit without pleasing. Despite his declaration on the side of pleasure, Rymer implies a didactic purpose for tragedy.

Since there are only minor differences between Rymer's approach to Beaumont and Fletcher and Jonson and his approach to Shakespeare, for the sake of avoiding repetition *The Tragedies of the Last Age* is treated here only insofar as this work serves to clarify Rymer's critical standards and method. Specific illustration of his tragic theory is restricted to his statements on *Othello*. In his examination of *Othello* in *A Short View of Tragedy*, for example, Rymer extracts three possible lessons from the plot: (1) Young ladies of high social station should not, without their parents' consent, elope with Moors; (2) Wives should keep track of their linen; (3) Husbands, before becoming jealous or violent, must have mathematical proof of their wives' infidelity. Rymer believes that the fable, or plot, *"the Soul of a Tragedy,"* should demonstrate a fairly complicated moral lesson, which must be infused into the whole texture of the play in such a way as to contribute to the pleasure of the audience. What moral lesson can be learned from *Othello*? asks Rymer. Is not its effect "to make us repine and grumble at Providence; and the government of the World? If this be our end, what boots it to be Vertuous?" (p. 161). Rymer's concern with the moral quality of tragedy is closely connected with his idea of poetic justice. *Othello* violates poetic justice and thus contributes nothing to moral utility.

Rymer, who was believed to have coined the phrase *poetical justice,* may possibly have derived the concept from Julius Caesar Scaliger, although the theory is also advocated by Rapin's commentary on Aristotle and by the French formalists generally.[15] Joseph Wood Krutch notes, however, that Sir Philip Sidney implies the theory of poetic justice in *The Defence of Poesie,* Ben Jonson also does so in the dedication of *Volpone,* and Dryden refers specifically to poetic justice in *An Essay of Dramatic Poesy.*[16] Rymer carried the concept to mathematical extremes. No character is to be permitted to commit more crimes than he can be punished for (p. 27). In *The Tragedies of the Last Age,* Rymer incorrectly ascribes the principle of poetic justice to the Greek dramatists. Sophocles and Euripides, says Rymer, realized that in history the righteous and the unjust come to the same end, virtue is oppressed, and wickedness thrives on the throne. Therefore, the particular truths of history are incapable of revealing universal and eternal truths. Such realities have perplexed the wisest and have been used by atheists to destroy confidence in Divine Providence.

---

15.   Spingarn, 1: lxxiii-lxxiv.
16.   Joseph Wood Krutch, *Comedy and Conscience after the Restoration* (New York: Columbia University Press, 1924), p. 79.

The poet, therefore, says Rymer, must necessarily present justice exactly administered if he wishes to please. He must teach by example in such a way as to give pleasure. Since people can scarcely reconcile the mystery of life's undeserved suffering with faith in God, whose ways are unsearchable, they cannot accept such an administration of justice by poets, who, they assume, are comprehensible. Rymer acknowledges that what is naturally unpleasant may give pleasure when well imitated, but this is only true of superficial deformities suitable for comedy. Disagreeing as he does in this respect with Aristotle, who in the *Poetics* had said that even what is painful in life when imitated gives pleasure, Rymer asserts that if the mind and heart are engaged, what is unpleasant in actuality can never please in imitation unless poetic justice is observed (pp. 22-23).[17]

Poetic justice is not an Aristotelian principle but a doctrine traceable to implications in Plato's *Republic*, Sec. I, Book iii, ix. 392B; in *Laws*, Book ii, 660E-661A-D; and in Horace's *Ars poetica*, ll. 196-201.[18] It owes something, also, to Aristotle's distributive justice, an idea that applies to ethical principles rather than to art. Aristotle does not, of course, permit in tragedy the downfall of a totally good man or the triumph of the wicked. For drama to achieve tragic catharsis, according to Aristotle, the hero must be a human being with virtues and weaknesses, suffering a downfall as the result of a fatal mistake in combination with unfortunate circumstances. The concept of poetic justice reflects the effect of the Renaissance epic principle of teaching by example and the resulting exaggerated stress on the poet's ethical function. Poetic justice almost requires the interpretation of nature as that of

17.   See Else, text of *Poetics*, iv. 48b10-15, pp. 124-25.
18.   *The Republic of Plato*, trans. with intro. and notes by Francis M. Cornford (New York: Oxford University Press, 1945), pp. 78-80. *Laws*, 2 vols., Trans. R.G. Bury in *Plato with an English Translation*, 10 vols. (London: W. Heinemann; New York: G.P. Putnam's Sons, 1926), 9: 114-17. Flacci Q. Horati, *Opera*, with previous annotations by Edward C. Wickham and current annotations by H.W. Garrod (London: Oxford University Press, 1963; first published 1901).

ideal nature favored by Rymer in *The Tragedies of the Last Age*.[19]

Louis I. Bredvold does not support the suggestion of Spingarn that the nature imitated in the later seventeenth century reflected either new scientific discoveries or the mechanical universe of Hobbes and Locke. He believes that this concept of nature may be much better understood from Cicero than from Hobbes. He traces the concept back to the Stoics, for whom "to follow Nature" was the secret of the good life. "To them Nature meant a kind of world-order, an order perceived by the enlightened and disciplined soul, which in turn found within itself a noble capacity for conforming to this ideal world-order, and thus raising itself above sordidness and vice. The Nature which is imitated by art is also of this ideal and normative kind." The formulators of literary doctrine in the later seventeenth century when they spoke of the imitation of nature meant, Bredvold believes, an ideal nature, "*la belle nature*." The conception did not represent an escape from actuality but an interpretation of it. "They believed that art must deal with reality, as opposed to unreality, and also as opposed to actuality."[20]

Rymer is under the impression that he identifies nature with what is rational and in accord with common sense. Much of the confusion in his criticism, however, results from his tendency to think at the same time that to imitate nature means to imitate the Platonic ideal or more usually the socially stylized type. What is rational and in accord with common sense may mean for Rymer what is normal, what is average, what is typical, or what ideally "should be." These aspects of nature, all distinct, become identified with one another. Rymer feels free to condemn the imitation of anything that cannot be placed within one of these categories, or sometimes within all of them at once, as the imitation of "deform'd" nature.

---

19.   Francis Gallaway. *Reason, Rule, and Revolt in English Classicism* (New York: C. Scribner's Sons, 1940), pp. 150-52.
20.   "Platonism in Neo-Classical Esthetics," *ELH* 1 (1934): 98-99.

One point on which Rymer's criticism exhibits a certain tension relates to his attempt to reconcile both what is reasonable in nature and what is demanded by poetic justice with the fate of the tragic hero. Rymer's support of the principle of poetic justice conflicts with his recognition that for pity to be felt an element of disproportion must be involved in the hero's downfall, a disproportion suggested in Greek tragedy by oblique references to the powerful and incomprehensible forces that determine man's destiny. Rymer was conscious of the dichotomy between the requirements of poetic justice and his belief that the hero's tragic flaw must be involuntary. How can the hero be made to suffer when he is not, strictly speaking, morally responsible for what happens? How can such an outcome be in accord with reason, and how can poetic justice be fairly administered in such a case? Rymer's realization of this problem leads him momentarily to a deeper-than-usual insight into the nature of decorum in the *Poetics*. Among the ancient tragic heroes, Rymer notes, there are no willful malefactors, for criminals cannot be objects of pity. Also, because to see an act of violence represented shocks the audience and decreases its capacity to feel pity, the Greeks avoided showing bloodshed on the stage. It was not that the ancients were unacquainted with violence, as Oedipus, Orestes, and Medea testify. ''But they took care to wash the Viper, to cleanse away the venom, and with such art to prepare the morsel: that they made it all Junket to the tast, and all Physick in the operation'' (p. 28). The Greeks, Rymer realizes, did not represent violence for its own sake or for the effect of its representation upon the audience, but showed its significance in such a way as to evoke an enlightening catharsis.

Rymer's comments on the tragic hero and on decorum in this case accurately reflect Aristotle, for whom the *hamartia* represents a mistake rather than a conscious act. Furthermore, Aristotle did not consider the *pathos* so important in arousing pity and fear as the realization on the part of the audience of the connection between the *hamartia* and the recognition. The emotional effect of tragedy is greatest, according to Aristotle, if the violent act is assumed to have been committed but is averted.

Certain assumptions are common both to *The Tragedies of the Last Age* and to *A Short View of Tragedy*. Both works support the "rules" of Aristotle on the basis of common sense. Both stress the unities as further deductions from common sense, although Rymer does not preoccupy himself with the unities, referring to them in *The Tragedies of the Last Age* as "the *mechanical part* of Tragedies," and regarding their violation in *Othello* as a minor absurdity without moral significance (pp. 18, 142). The instruction offered by the plot and the revelation of the workings of poetic justice are more important to Rymer than what he considers the minor technicalities in a play. Nonetheless, he ridicules the fact that the audience must make a journey from Venice to Cyprus in *Othello*, although "we have no *Moses* to bid the Waters *make way*," as in the mystery plays (p. 142).

A Short View of Tragedy, in contrast to *The Tragedies of the Last Age*, refers less to nature as the ideal and more to nature as the typical or average. The influence of Horace predominates, together with the tendency in Buckingham's *Rehearsal* to ridicule by the standard of common sense any action or speech that goes beyond the ordinary. Rymer's criticism of *Othello* uses much the same procedure that he applied to Beaumont and Fletcher's plays in *The Tragedies of the Last Age*, except that instead of making comparative references to Greek plays he cites Horace as an authority and makes no suggestion for revising the play.

Rymer displays a radical departure from Aristotle in *A Short View of Tragedy* by calling the chorus "the root and original" and "most necessary part" of tragedy (p. 84). He defends the use of the chorus chiefly because he associates it with the origin of Greek tragedy, and because he finds it a characteristic of model ancient tragedies. The chorus, he believes, is the basis of verisimilitude; it also insures a reasonable observance of the unities. He is aware, too, as Aristotle was, of the value of the chorus as a "goodly show" in attracting the interest of the audience.

Besides upholding the use of the chorus, Rymer is most insistent upon the observance of his view of probability in tragedy. "*Poetry,*"said Rymer in the Preface to Rapin, "has no life, nor can have any operation without *probability:* it may indeed amuse the People, but moves not the *Wise,* for whom alone (according to *Pythagoras*) it is ordain'd" (p. 8). Probability means for Rymer the logical, factual connection between events and character in tragedy that common sense can follow without recourse to psychological probing or sophisticated perception. His belief that persons represented in tragedy must demonstrate the logical behavior assumed to characterize either ideal or, as in the case of *Othello,* more or less normal, typical human beings indicates his inattention to Aristotle's remarks on "plausible impossibilities" in plot and "consistently inconsistent" characters. As a result, he is insensitive to the ambiguities in human behavior that can only be realized by means of feeling, imagination, and life experience. The idiosyncrasies of historical characters, says Rymer in *The Tragedies of the Last Age*, may legitimately be represented in tragedy, but invented characters must conform to "*general probability*" (p. 24). A "wise" audience will be interested in the rational development of plot and character, and will reject any unnecessary display of crude human passion or violence. Some discernible logic must direct the behavior of characters in tragedy even when they express hate, love, remorse, or grief. The effect of tragedy in relation to a select audience is always Rymer's concern. He follows the Horatian principle that the common people's opinions of poets are seldom true and not to be sought after. Although he thinks that taste should be guided by what has pleased the judicious down through the ages, this *consensus gentium* means for him the judgments of rational and discriminating minds. Tragedy, he believes, should appeal more to the analytical intelligence of the audience than to feeling and imagination. Tragedy, he says, requires a *"purging* of the *passions,"* but this purgation is achieved by seeing the workings of poetic justice in the plot (p. 75). Passion should be kept within the bounds of reason and decorum.

Rationalism created a rigid separation between the imaginative and emotional responses in man and what he was expected to know as a logical, thinking person. It is therefore contrary to common sense to think that a Venetian senator's daughter would elope with a Moor, that the senators would be interested in her case and sympathetic toward her, that an army officer would intentionally conspire to make his superior officer jealous, and that a chain of accidental, even trivial, circumstances would end in her murder. If we for some reason feel that such events are possible and are moved to pity and fear by them, we lack common sense. In a rational universe, such things do not happen, and if they do they are of no moral significance to society as a whole. Rymer's emotional responses are directed by common sense and propriety.

Antipathetic, as he is, to the "gothic" and romantic, Rymer objects to Shakespeare's choice of subject matter in *Othello*. He considers Giraldi Cinthio's novella an unsuitable source for tragedy, and he disapproves of Shakespeare's innovation in choosing to adapt the material of romance to tragedy. A man with an ancient rather than a modern consciousness in his attitude toward romantic love, Rymer considers it too inconsequential a matter to form the central interest in tragedy.

H. B. Charlton in *Shakespearian Tragedy* has pointed out that Cinthio's principles of tragedy were on the whole an adaptation of Seneca's. In *The Tragedies of the Last Age,* Rymer condemns Seneca's unnatural way of writing, his sensationalism, and emphasis on violence. Seneca, he states, copied the thoughts of Sophocles and Euripides, but demonstrated little of their "good sense" (p. 57). Shakespearean tragedy, influenced by the Senecan tradition (though rendering its violence and passion meaningful), is judged by Rymer in terms of a rigid interpretation of the classical dramatic form.

Cinthio, says Charlton, argued that tragedy must "reflect a range of experience and base itself on a system of values which are felt by its audience to be real." Tragedy, consequently, should take its material not from ancient mythology or recorded history, for these portray a world that may appear remote to the audience. The plots most suitable for modern tragedy, according to Cinthio, are to be found in modern fiction: "For modern fiction," says Charlton, "is the mythology of to-day. It is the corpus of story through which the world appears as it seems to be to living men; it mirrors accepted codes of conduct, displays the particular manner of contemporary consciousness, and adopts the current assumptions of human values."[21] One notable difference between the ancient and modern consciousness lies in the value placed on love of man for woman. Since 1200 A.D. love has become a subject of almost compulsive interest and is often regarded as the most intense human experience. Modern fiction revolves around love. Dramatists, like Shakespeare, who took their plots from fiction also took over love as the main interest in their plays. Seven of Cinthio's own nine plays take their plots from novels, and the remaining two present famous classical love stories, *Dido* and *Cleopatra*. Cinthio's practice prevailed to such an extent that sixteenth-century tragedy turned to novels as a source of subject matter, despite the protests of traditionalists. Shakespeare followed the new direction in *Othello*.

Rymer summarizes what he considers the improbable sequence of events by which Shakespeare's play develops:

> *Othello* the night of his arrival at *Cyprus,* is to consummate with *Desdemona,* they go to Bed. Both are rais'd and run into the Town amidst the Souldiers that were a fighting: then go to Bed again, that morning he sees *Cassio* with her; She importunes him to restore

---

21. *Shakespearian Tragedy* (Cambridge: University Press, 1949), pp. 49-50.

Cassio. Othello shews nothing of the Souldiers Mettle: but like a tedious, drawling, tame Goose, is gaping after any paultrey insinuation, labouring to be jealous; and catching at every blown surmize (p. 149).

The foundation or plot of the play, Rymer concludes, is monstrous or unnatural. Reason, which is common to all men, must be the poet's guide, states Rymer in *The Tragedies of the Last Age,* for reason will never permit the poet to deviate from what is natural. If he abandons himself to fancy, on the other hand, his fancy may be "monstrous," or singular, and please no one but himself (p. 62). The effect of *Othello* upon the audience, according to Rymer, is one of horror and aversion, not of pity "or any passion Tragical and Reasonable" (p. 150). It is not unusual to assume, said Rymer in *The Tragedies of the Last Age,* that what is customary corresponds to what is natural, but the poet must be a philosopher, not an historian.He must not "take *Nature* at the *second hand,* soyl'd and deform'd as it passes in the customes of the unthinking vulgar" (p. 62). Rymer disapproves of the plot of *Othello* as an epitome of human experience. It is too eccentric.Nature is identified here by Rymer with what he considers the normal and the general as opposed to exceptional deviations from common conduct.

The rule of probability confirms the concept of decorum. The later seventeenth-century concept of decorum referred particularly to the manners of figures in drama. In the tradition of Horace, manners were regarded as differing according to inborn disposition, age, sex, climate, or social condition. Consistency between the manners and actions of characters must be readily apparent. Manners must also coincide with the traditional reputation of a historical or fictional character and not deviate in adherence to the conception first presented. Manners were considered clearest and probability best preserved if each character exhibited a ruling passion and if complexity and subtlety were avoided.

Rymer cannot reconcile Shakespeare's reference to *"supersubtle venetians"* with the character of "the noble *Desdemona,"* in whom he can find nothing "that is not below any Countrey Chamber-maid with us" (p. 134). Shakespeare's portrayal of Venetian noblemen and of the Venetian senate, likewise, violates probability.

Neither in his actions nor in his reputation does Othello exhibit the qualities of a general, says Rymer, except perhaps in killing himself. Contrary to the normal instincts of a military officer, he appoints Iago to kill Cassio, and "chuses himself to murder the silly Woman his Wife, that was like to make no resistance" (p. 134). Love and jealousy, furthermore, are not consistent with a soldier's character, states Rymer, except in comedy.

Iago is an even more intolerable character—"never in Tragedy, nor in Comedy, nor in Nature was a Souldier with his Character" (p. 134). He does not correspond with Horace's description of a soldier.[22] In Shakespeare's own words, says Rymer, Iago is a villain, rogue, and *"couzening Slave, to get some Office"* (p. 135). Shakespeare himself knew that his character of Iago was inconsistent, states Rymer, but "to entertain the Audience with something new and surprising, against common sense, and Nature, he would pass upon us a close, dissembling, false, insinuating rascal, instead of an open-hearted, frank, plain-dealing Souldier, a character constantly worn by them for some thousands of years in the World" (p. 135). Iago's behavior does not resemble that of English army officers, who "when disgusted by the Captain, throw up their Commissions, bluster, and are bare-fac'd" (p. 135). Rymer cannot bring himself to believe that the character

---

22. Horace enumerated types of dramatic characters and described from rhetoric the speech techniques appropriate to their social status. Rymer's approach to Aristotle's comments on the parts of tragedy strongly suggests Horace's rhetorical influence, an influence that led to stylistic formalism and to the concept of tragedy as a work to be assembled by consciously acquired techniques.

of Iago is at all reconcilable with the Venetians' conception of military men. Iago is not simple and honest as a typical soldier should be. Rymer fails to appreciate the tragic irony of Iago's appearing to be precisely that.

Referring to what he considers the unnatural quality of Iago's character, Rymer points out that Iago had some reason to have a grudge against Othello and Cassio, but Desdemona had done him no harm. On the contrary, she had been gracious to him and his wife. She was his compatriot, a young woman of noble family. For Iago to be an accomplice to her murder "shews nothing of a Souldier, nothing of a Man, nothing of Nature in it" (p. 155). Iago is a monster. "Can it be any diversion," asks Rymer, "to see a Rogue beyond what the Devil ever finish'd? Or wou'd it be any instruction to an Audience?" (p. 156).

In Desdemona we have, according to Rymer, not a Venetian lady but a fool. Her elopement and her pleas on behalf of Cassio "the very night she Beds" Othello are incredible (p. 135). Rymer concludes that there is nothing in the characters of *Othello* "either for the profit or to delight an Audience" (p. 136). Rymer's estimate of the characters in *Othello* shows his preoccupation with the social effects of tragedy. Aristotle, however, was concerned not with the representation of ideal characters or of the typical or average but with the depiction of consistent characters. The concept of decorum with emphasis on the ideal, Rymer took from the French formalists, La Mesnardière and L'Abbé d'Aubignac. Although he places more stress on ideal characterization in *The Tragedies of the Last Age,* whereas he is more concerned with the typical or average in *A Short View of Tragedy,* the fact is that he often confuses or mingles all three categories in his critical analysis of this aspect of the play.

Reason and the imitation of nature interpreted rationalistically explain Rymer's internal decorum (meaning consistency in characterization)—the object of which is verisimilitude. The French formalists transformed Aristotle's insistence that a character be logically developed into a system of rigid rules. Since many of the attitudes of Rymer are similar to La Mesnardière's, especially the relation of court etiquette to the application of decorum, Rymer elaborates the rules in *The Tragedies of the Last Age*, stating that no woman is to kill a man, no servant a master, and no subject a king.[23] Aristotle implied that a character's actions, though they may at times be inconsistent, should have an ultimate psychological consistency, however complex, whereas Rymer and La Mesnardière mean that they must be consistent with the conventionally expected behavior of formally defined types.

The typical character can be imitated from nature, but the typical must also, in Rymer's view, have qualities of the ideal, particularly of the courtly ideal. Decorum, as a result, becomes external; that is, it must conform with the way the contemporary world wished to see itself presented. The rule of external decorum leads to a moral end. Only virtuous characters, models of behavior, demand sympathy; evil and low characters are excluded from tragedy.[24] External decorum is applied by Rymer not only to the characters and actions of tragedy but to tragedy as a type of drama. It must deal with people of high social station, who, no matter what the time or setting, observe the stylized conventions of elegant society.

Rymer concludes his analysis of plot and character by referring to the second scene of Act Five, in which Othello at the moment of murdering Desdemona "is as careful of her Souls health, as it had been her *Father Confessor,*" noting that Desdemona speaks even after she has been smothered to death, another instance in which the play violates nature and probability (pp. 160-61).

Rymer's consideration of the thoughts in *Othello* is guided by the principle he enunciated in *The Tragedies of the Last Age*:

---

23.   See G.B. Dutton, "The French Formalists and Thomas Rymer," *PMLA* 29 (1914): 162-63.
24.   See diss. by Dollard, pp. 174-77.

"Tragedy requires not what is only Natural, but what is great in Nature, and such thoughts as quality and Court-education might inspire" (p. 35). By this standard of decorum Rymer concludes that the characters in *Othello* cannot offer many thoughts "that are either true, or fine, or noble" (p. 136). Rymer indicates that the thoughts expressed in tragedy must be edifying and reflect courtly attitudes. Aristotle, in contrast, was concerned with thoughts as expressing character. The speeches of characters, according to Aristotle, may reflect either the ethical or intellectual aspect of the characters. Certainly the speeches of the characters in *Othello* reflect very fully the moral attitudes of the characters and their ways of reasoning. Aristotle did not mean that thoughts should express ideal or even valid ethical standards or syllogistic reasoning processes. Aristotle meant that the thoughts expressed by the speeches of the characters in tragedy should reveal the ethical and intellectual experiences peculiar to each character. Thoughts, in other words, according to Aristotle, demonstrate character, but not ideal character.

From an examination of the thoughts in the play, Rymer proceeds to a discussion of the expression, although he feels that without suitable thoughts the expression does not merit separate consideration: "In the *Neighing* of an Horse, or in the *growling* of a Mastiff, there is a meaning, there is as lively expression, and, may I say, more humanity, than many times in the Tragical flights of *Shakespear*" (p. 136).

Rymer ridicules the elegance of Cassio's diction as inappropriate to an army officer, and points to the improbability of the exchanges of wit among Cassio, Iago, and Desdemona at a time when they have just escaped a destructive storm, when Desdemona may at any moment expect news about whether her bridegroom has survived or perished, and when Cyprus is a city tensely awaiting enemy attack. This sort of quibbling Rymer compares to the custom of strolling players who interlarded scriptural plays with "Drolls" and "Fooleries," and thereby pleased the rabble who paid them money. "These Carpenters and Coblers were the guides he followed'' (p. 145). Copying such models, says Rymer, accounts for the farce and extraneous matter in Shakespeare's tragedies. Rymer's comment shows that he rejects any model for tragedy except the classical. The introduction of word play for its own sake into tragedy abuses the theater and profanes tragedy, Rymer believes. Rymer's attack upon the improbable conversation of Desdemona, Iago, and Cassio at the time of their arrival at Cyprus overlooks what may have been Shakespeare's intention—to show elegant young people exhibiting nonchalance, or *sprezzatura,* at a moment of crisis. Interpreted in the light of Shakespeare's keen observation of human nature, the witty exchanges in the scene are in accord with the psychology of men and women who must demonstrate grace under pressure.

Referring to Iago's suggestion of the sexual relationship between Desdemona and Cassio, Rymer asks whether a general and his sub-officer—Venetians, soldiers, and officers—would be apt to speak in language such as they use. When Iago, says Rymer, leads Othello into the ruse of observing Cassio, ''*Othello* is as wise a commentator, and makes his applications pat, as heart cou'd wish—but I wou'd not expect to find this Scene acted nearer than in *Southwark* Fair. But the *Hankerchief* is brought in at last, to stop all holes, and close the evidence'' (p. 155). With such proof, Othello and Iago decide that the offenders must be murdered. Rymer, in this instance, judges the dialogue of Othello and Iago according to the standard of external decorum, or the expected behavior of men in military life. By the standard of internal decorum, that is, consistency of characterization, it is not impossible that officers might express the feelings of Iago and Othello in language that gives the same psychological effect as the language heightened by art that Shakespeare uses. Dialogue in drama is not a mere reproduction of dialogue in life. The playwright may use any method he chooses if the effect is convincing.

Rymer criticizes the individual thoughts in the play as inconsistent. The lines of Othello bidding farewell to the ''*Pride, Pomp, and Circumstance of glorious War*'' (III, iii, 358), are recited,

Rymer contends, only for the sake of the pleasing sound. "Yet this sort of imagery and amplification is extreamly taking, where it is just and natural" (p. 152), he says, making reference to a similar passage in *Gorboduc,* the fable of which, he had claimed earlier, in discussing English drama, might have been a better model for Shakespeare and Ben Jonson "than any guide they have had the luck to follow" (p. 130).

In the exchange between Othello and Iago (III, iii, 94ff.), Rymer believes, the words actually impede the effect of the action "as either forc'd, or heavy, or trifling, or incoherent, or improper, or most what improbable" (p. 149). Without the words, the dramatic suspense would be greater. "When no words interpose to spoil the conceipt, every one interprets as he likes best" (p. 149). Only the theatrical element has made this scene in *Othello* popular, says Rymer. "It is purely from the *Action*; from the Mops and the Mows, the Grimace, the Grins and Gesticulation. Such scenes as this have made all the World run after *Harlequin* and *Scaramuccio*" (p. 149). Rymer believed, as did Aristotle, that the least important part of tragedy is the spectacle. Nor did he think that the excellence of tragedy should be judged by the actors' performances. Rymer insists in *The Tragedies of the Last Age* upon a distinction between what pleases in itself "and what *pleases* upon the account of *Machines, Actors, Dances* and circumstances which are meerly *accidental* to the *Tragedy*" (p. 19).

Rymer was interested in establishing in English tragedy the conventions of classical Greek drama as interpreted by the French critics. What Rymer overlooks is the tradition and genres of romantic art. Because no formalized Elizabethan literary criticism existed, there was little perception of the dramatic conventions emerging from the popular or "people's drama"—conventions long in existence.

Shakespeare's Othello, for example, resembles in some respects the hero of romance who is above other men and his environment by reason of his position, whose actions are superhuman, but who is himself a human being. "The hero of romance moves in a world in which the ordinary laws of nature are slightly suspended." He performs acts of prodigious courage and possesses magic talismans that are not contrary to probability once the conventions of romance have been accepted.[25] Romance permits the writer to present the truths of human experience under circumstances of the writer's own choice or creation. Othello's adventures and "hairbreadth scapes" are reminiscent of the exploits of the hero of romance. The handkerchief is like a magic talisman. Naïve drama usually chooses some kind of romance as subject matter, and it must be remembered that Shakespeare's drama springs from primitive English drama and from Seneca.

The romance, tending as it does to be introverted and personal, deals with characters subjectively.[26] Neoclassical standards of drama stressed order, clarity, and unambiguous form. The writer of prose romance does not create realistic characters, says Northrop Frye, so much as figures that resemble "psychological archetypes." The quest of romance involves a conflict between a hero and some demonic antagonist. "It is in the romance that we find Jung's libido, anima, and shadow reflected in the hero, heroine, and villain respectively." Romance as a consequence often exhibits a "subjective intensity."[27]

Effective drama is firmly rooted in human psychology, and, no matter how bizarre or unrealistic its subject matter, this basic relationship can never be severed. The ordinary spectator responds psychologically to drama, even when he cannot understand the play and is ignorant of dramatic conventions. Domestic tragedy is particularly psychological in emphasis, and *Othello* is in many ways a domestic tragedy, dealing with the particular relationship of individuals. Neoclassical critics ignored the fact that the particular always has aspects of the universal.[28]

---

25.   Northrop Frye, *Anatomy of Criticism* (Princeton, N.J.: Princeton University Press, 1957), p. 33.
26.   *Ibid.*, p. 308.
27.   *Ibid.*, p. 304.
28.   See W. K. Wimsatt, Jr., "The Structure of the Concrete Universal in Literature," *PMLA* 62 (March 1947): 264-80.

Rymer's judgments on the plot and characters of *Othello* are based almost exclusively on the standards of probability, external decorum, and moral utility. Desdemona, the senators, Iago, and Othello do not live and behave as Rymer assumes persons of their respective ranks would do.

Supporting the idea of tragedy as a school of manners, Rymer applies the standards of common sense and rigid, neoclassical rules to *Othello,* despite the fact that Shakespeare's play emerged from a popular romantic tradition unconnected with classical drama. According to these standards, he finds the plot of the play contrary to nature and probability (narrowly interpreted), the characters unnatural and improper, the thoughts uninspired or inappropriate, and the expression disconnected from the action or contrary to verisimilitude.

It must be admitted that Rymer makes us realize the problems of technical structure and of convention in drama. Undoubtedly, by the late seventeenth century, the spirit of the age demanded a tighter form and unity in English drama. Without a genius such as Shakespeare, at a time when rationalism was predominant, tragedy was inevitably destined to die or to take a new direction.

Othello can much more easily be reconciled with Aristotle's own theory of tragedy than with Rymer's. Othello's *hamartia* leads to the reversal of his expected happy fulfillment in marriage. He mistakes Desdemona for what she is not, commits a fatal act, and recognizes his error. Pity and fear are aroused and to some extent purged, although there is a good deal of the *alazon* or tragic impostor in Othello, who first appears better than other men because he does not recognize the irrational potentialities of his own nature, as Sophocles' Oedipus and Euripides'characters do not.[29]

In making plot the vital element in tragedy, Rymer superficially

---

29.   Frye, p. 39.

follows Aristotle, but plot is not, Rymer failed to see, the story or myth. More accurately, "plot is something fuller and subtler than this; it is the way in which the action works itself out, the whole causal chain which leads to the final outcome."[30] Rymer's psychological perception is limited by his emphasis on common sense and on nature as the average or typical—an average or typical that must at the same time incorporate aspects of the ideal, in the sense of the courtly ideal.

Obviously *Othello* does not conform to the rules of neoclassical tragedy. The plot demands more psychological acumen than common sense can summon. The play certainly does not illustrate the workings of Providence, as this supernatural directing force is expected to work. The unities of time and place are not observed, although there is unity of action. The manners and actions of the characters are not apparently consistent, although they are "consistently inconsistent," and therefore in accord with Aristotle's own theory. The characters neither provide models of conduct, nor illustrate the conventions of neoclassical decorum. Furthermore, Shakespeare includes evil and low characters in *Othello,* and chooses not to maintain a clear and distinct proportion in the play.

Rymer's pronouncements on *Othello* demonstrate his rationalistic view of nature, his lack of psychological subtlety, and the hazards of approaching a work of art through any set of inflexible preconceptions. Shakespeare's play examined by Rymer's standards and method must be seen as a "bloody farce," in the sense of empty show made pretentious and palatable by elaborate stuffing and seasoning.

Each particular critical method tends to lead inevitably to certain evaluations of literary works. Rymer's criticism reveals little tension, except for his attempt to explain the problem involved in making the fate of the Aristotelian hero compatible with reason

---

30. David Daiches, *Critical Approaches to Literature* (Englewood Cliffs, N.J.: Prentice-Hall, Inc., 1956), p. 28.

and poetic justice. He is single-eyed in searching out in *Othello* the deviations from the standards of ancient, classical tragedy as he understands them. However, Rymer's method calls attention to aspects of Shakespeare's play that have escaped notice in other critical systems. Thus Rymer in his own way expands our critical consciousness—at least, from a historical point of view.

3

John Dennis's Theory of Tragedy: Shakespeare—"One of the Greatest Genius's That the World 'Er Saw for the Tragic Stage."

Although interested, as Rymer was, in the subject matter of tragedy and in the demands of the work itself, John Dennis gives more attention to the psychology of the artist and to the effect of tragedy upon the audience. His approach reveals greater historical perspective than that of Rymer, in consequence of which he is able to appreciate Shakespeare, as Rymer was not.

Dennis's most liberating critical innovation in relation to the artist is his idea of genius, first defined in the Preface to *Remarks upon "Prince Arthur"* (1696) as "the expression of a Furious Joy, or Pride, or Astonishment, or all of them caused by the conception of an extraordinary hint."[1] Dennis's definition of the classical *furor poeticus* is partly derived from Boileau's translation in 1674 of Longinus's *Peri Hupsous*. Longinus mentions two qualities of the sublime that result exclusively from the poet's innate ability rather than from art, namely, the capacity to form daring and magnificent thoughts and images, and the power

---

1. *The Critical Works of John Dennis*, ed. Edward Niles Hooker, 2 vols. (Baltimore: Johns Hopkins Press, 1939, 1943), 1:47. Citations from Dennis are from this two-volume edition.

to experience violent or even enthusiastic passions proceeding
from these thoughts and images.[2]

Dennis's theory of genius also bears a relationship to general
Hobbesian doctrine. Hobbes, in *Leviathan,* (1:viii), indicates that
the foundation of genius is passion, as it is for Dennis. One kind
of joy, according to Hobbes (*Leviathan* 1:vi), springs from a
sudden exaltation of the mind in its own power. Dennis, beginning with Hobbes's doctrine of the exaltation of the soul in composition, stated that the frenzy of the poet, which had formerly
been considered divine, is either a common passion or a "complication of common Passions" (1:46). The Preface to *Remarks
upon "Prince Arthur"* expresses Dennis's views on the nature of
poetic genius and on the sources of poetic inspiration. The capacity to write well and easily, says Dennis, springs from the same
sources as other kinds of happiness in ordinary life. The soul becomes exalted by a hint peculiarly its own. If the hint is great
and elevated, the soul expands at the sudden realization of its
own unique power. A man in such a state of exaltation expresses
himself differently from one who is serene (1:46-47).

For the genius, poetic composition is an intuitive act that
simultaneously brings together strong feeling and the figurative
language by which to express what the poet wants to say.[3] Poetic
creativity, Dennis holds, is marked by a kind of spontaneous,
organic unity. In *The Advancement and Reformation of Modern
Poetry* (1701), Dennis identifies this quality of genius with the
ability both to feel and to express passion. The successful
dramatist, for instance, is one who is able to portray strong passion rather than one who constructs a well-made plot. Dennis
denies, however, that genius alone is sufficient to achieve a work

---

2. *Dionysius Longinus On the Sublime,* trans. from the Greek by William Smith, D.D.,
4th ed. (London, 1770), in Samuel H. Monk, *The Sublime: A Study of Critical Theories
in XVIII-Century England,* (Ann Arbor, Mich.: University of Michigan Press, 1960),
p. 13. (First published New York: Modern Language Association of America, 1935.)
3.   Dennis (1943), 2:xcvi. See idem, 1:2.

of stature: "Yet 'tis Art," he writes, "that makes a Subject very great, and, consequently, gives Occasion for a great Genius to shew itself" (1:229). Without the control of established literary conventions, especially in tragedy and the epic, Dennis believes, poetic chaos will inevitably prevail. He insists that poetic fury be tempered by judgment, although he speaks of the forces of nature prevailing in the poet, even sometimes exalting him to the divine.

Dennis, as does Hobbes, defines vivid thoughts by calling them images. For Dennis, imagery means the material from reflection. The imagination for him is not limited to the mere power to recall images, however, or to invent a fanciful combination of images. It has aspects of a creative faculty, for as Clarence D. Thorpe notes:

> With Dennis, as with Hobbes, ideas have their origin in sense impression. These ideas are of two sorts: those which come from ordinary objects and those which derive from the uncommon and the extraordinary. In the first case the ideas are full and clear; in the second, they are indefinite, somewhat beyond the realm of full apprehension. The first give rise to ordinary passions, the second to the enthusiastic passions.[4]

Dennis originally made this distinction between the ordinary and enthusiastic passions in *The Advancement and Reformation of Modern Poetry*. Three years later, in *The Grounds of Criticism in Poetry* (1704), he changed the term "ordinary" to "vulgar," and once more defined the vulgar and enthusiastic passions. Vulgar passions, giving rise to anger, pity, admiration, or wonder, are those aroused by objects themselves or by ideas in the ordinary course of life. The enthusiastic passions, leading to admiration, terror, horror, joy, sadness, or desire, are aroused by things outside common life. The enthusiastic passions are heightened by the mind's own consciousness of intense reflection. They are

---

4. *The Aesthetic Theory of Thomas Hobbes* (New York: Russell & Russell, 1964), pp. 230-31. (First published Ann Arbor, Mich.: University of Michigan Press, 1940.)

"caus'd by Ideas occurring to us in Meditation, and producing
the same Passions that the Objects of those Ideas would raise in
us, if they were set before us in the same light that those Ideas
give us of them" (1: 338-39). Enthusiastic passions are moved by
ideas of objects not as they actually appear to the senses but as
they are shaped and changed and interpreted by the human mind.
"Poetical Enthusiasm," said Dennis in *The Advancement and
Reformation of Modern Poetry,* "is a Passion guided by Judgment, whose Cause is not comprehended by us" (1: 217). It is
greater and more intense than ordinary passion. Illustrating the
difference between the vulgar and enthusiastic passions in *The
Grounds of Criticism in Poetry,* Dennis calls attention to the
difference between the minimal effect upon the imagination of
ordinary ideas in conversation and their power in meditation to
arouse terror, admiration, or horror (1: 339). Dennis's view of
the origin of poetic creativity in this respect resembles
Wordsworth's, but is different in that it emphasizes poetic fury
rather than "emotion recollected in tranquillity."

Dennis changed his original definition of genius as the expression of strong feeling caused by "an extraordinary hint," contained in *Remarks upon "Prince Arthur,"* to the one he offers in
The Advancement and Reformation of Modern Poetry, in which
genius in the poet means the power worthily to express great
passion, whether ordinary or enthusiastic, because he recognized
that tragedy deals with the ordinary passions. Poetry arouses both
vulgar and enthusiastic passions, states Dennis in *The Grounds of
Criticism in Poetry,* but the vulgar passions are preferable in a
way, because the poet who stirs these passions communicates to
the largest audience. The enthusiastic passions are more subtle,
and some people are incapable of experiencing them. The vulgar
passions must particularly predominate in the parts of the epic
and tragedy in which the characters converse together. Perhaps,
says Dennis, the wide appeal of the vulgar passions accounts for
Aristotle's preferring tragedy to the epic: "because the Vulgar

Passions prevail more in it, and are more violently moved in it; and therefore Tragedy must necessarily both please and instruct, more generally than Epick Poetry'' (1:339).

Dennis believed that since all knowledge proceeds from the senses, nearly all normal men are capable of experiencing what any man can experience. He denied any supernatural element to genius. But genius demands fine organs of perception and memory and the ability to form extraordinary thoughts and images. It requires also ''a degree of Fire sufficient to give their animal spirits a sudden and swift agitation'' (1:47). Only agitation can save the imagination from sterility. Dennis was influenced by Boileau and Rapin in deciding that agitation is produced by variety and surprise. The imitation of existing works, he believed, destroys surprise (2:civ-cv). Genius ultimately means for Dennis the power adequately to express great passion. It includes also a balanced relationship between passion and judgment. Because, in the genius, the fire of the heart and the fire of the mind are one, Dennis suggests, such a poet will express himself passionately, and give his finished work the unity of a living organism.

Dennis's view of genius and his conviction that poetry results from passion controlled by judgment are related to his philosophy of pleasure. In *The Usefulness of the Stage* (1698), Dennis states that the end of man is to achieve happiness, defined by Dennis as pleasure. It is by this principle that God maintains harmony in the universe. Happiness, he says, eludes men because they have associated it with the life of reason, and have, as a consequence, negated the importance of strong feeling. Pleasure, on the contrary, results, says Dennis, from passion—from being moved. In life, the most basic pleasure is that of sense, aroused by desire, but happiness after death will mean a state of ecstatic, intuitive knowledge, not dependent on the process of reason. Although reason, therefore, is not the basic or ultimate source of happiness, nonetheless man can never be happy when he ignores or violates it, because by nature he is intended to be a rational being. No passion, then, can be in harmony with the will, except a passion approved by the understanding. Such a passion must have authentic sources and be increased by proportionate degrees. Similarly, the passions aroused by tragedy must be authentic and proportionate: "Thus are they mov'd, thus are they rais'd in every well-writ Tragedy," Dennis writes, "till they come to as great a Height as Reason can very well bear. Besides, the very Motion has a Tendency to the subjecting them to Reason, and the very Raising purges and moderates them. So that the Passions are seldom any where so pleasing and no where so safe, as they are in Tragedy" (1:150-51).

Passion, according to Dennis, is pleasurable, but requires a check by reason. Dennis, although at first under the influence of the fabulist André Dacier, was the chief English proponent of Descartes's view that the stirring of passion is itself a kind of interior sensuality. Pleasure arises from the physical stimulus of animal spirits, provided that the resulting movement is harmonious. According to the theory of tragic pleasure derived from Descartes, the motion of the passions alone arouses pleasure and pity and fear, but the effect is modified by our realization that the experience of the play is not identical with the experience of actual life.[5] The agitation and release of passion that we experience when witnessing a tragedy account for its pleasurable effect; even the sight of what is painful in actual life can please us in imitation, because the effect of what we experience is tempered by the controlling power of art. Seeing a tragedy brings the passions into harmony with reason, psychic balance is thus restored, and man is more able as a consequence to act morally. Dennis was also influenced by the concept stemming from Book

---

5. Earl Wasserman, "The Pleasures of Tragedy," *ELH* 14 (1947): 288-89. See Baxter Hathaway, "The Lucretian 'Return upon Ourselves' in Eighteenth Century Theories of Tragedy," *PMLA* 62 (September 1947): 672-76.

II of Lucretius's *De rerum natura,* that pleasure is associated with the viewer's realization of his own freedom from similar suffering.

Dennis sees the ends of poetry and of tragedy as the conventional ones of moral utility and pleasure. Poetry, says Dennis in *The Grounds of Criticism in Poetry,* is "an Art, by which a Poet excites Passion (and for that very Cause entertains Sense) in order to satisfy and improve, to delight and reform the Mind, and so to make Mankind happier and better: from which it appears that Poetry has two Ends, a subordinate, and a final one; the subordinate one is Pleasure, and the final one is Instruction" (1:336). In the tradition of Sir Philip Sidney, Dennis believed that poetry moves us not only to want to know what is virtuous but also to want to act virtuously. Even the moral philosopher, says Dennis, cannot reform without appealing to the passionate side of man's nature. However, because poetry moves more than philosophy, it also has greater power to reform. On the basis of this reasoning, Dennis concludes that the fable, incidents, characters, sentiments, and expression in tragedy must be especially designed to move, and that since tragedy moves more than comedy, it is consequently more instructive.

Referring to Aristotle, Dennis stresses the emotional effect of surprise in tragedy, particularly in the peripety. The surprise, says Dennis, following Aristotle, should appear to result from necessity and not from chance.

> Tragedy, says *Aristotle* in his *Poetick,* is the Imitation of an Action which excites Compassion and Terror. Now these two Passions proceed from Surprize, when the Incidents spring from one another against our Expectation: For those Incidents, continues the Philosopher, are always more admirable, than those which arrive by Chance; which is evident from this, says he, That even of accidental Things, those are always the most Wonderful and most Surprizing, which at the same Time that they arrive by Chance, seem to fall out by Design, and by a certain particular Secret Conduct. (1:230)

Surprise is most effective when related to a pattern of apparent order. If the opponents of regularity would study Sophocles' *Oedipus,* Dennis had previously said, they would see how the structure of the play leads from surprise to surprise, from compassion to terror, and from terror to compassion again (1:201). Experience and philosophy have shown, says Dennis, that regularity of structure is required "for the surer exciting of Passion" (1:200).

The Advancement and Reformation of Modern Poetry connects tragedy closely with religious experience, and notes the religious origin of Greek tragedy. Both religion (meaning for Dennis Christianity) and poetry stimulate our passions and at the same time enable us to harmonize our passions with our reason and will. Religion for the believing Christian, Dennis suggests, implies a rational order controlling the universe, an order also manifested in the design of the poet's work, even though the poet may happen to be an ancient Greek rather than a modern Christian. Just as the Christian's belief that the turbulence of life and history will ultimately be rendered meaningful by a just God enables him to control his passions, without repressing them, so the essential regularity of the dramatist's work makes our response to tragedy enlightening and harmonious, whereas it might otherwise be frenzied and disjointed.

The moderns, who have equaled the ancients in satire and surpassed them in comedy, have fallen below them in tragedy, according to Dennis, because they have failed to use the resources of Christianity as the Greeks used those of their religion. Dennis, more than Rymer or Dryden, comes close to grasping the mythical nature of Greek tragedy, but his insight is unfortunately clouded by his conviction that tragedy must illustrate a moral allegory in terms of poetic justice.

Although the vulgar passions, associated with ordinary human experience, are the essential province of tragedy, Dennis believes, the enthusiastic passions—especially terror, associated with the extraordinary and the Divine—are helpful in achieving the end of moral utility. They also heighten the sense of the wonderful. All passions, Dennis believes, are based on self-love. Terror and compassion are aroused by calamities to our equals, persons in like circumstances, with like faults or faults to which we are susceptible. The more their calamities are related to a sense of the Divine and seem to result from Providence, the more wonderful, terrible, and moving they are. "And therefore a Train of Incidents," he writes, "which, contrary to our Expectation, surprizingly produce one another, is necessary, because the more plainly the Punishment appears the Result of the Faults, and the more clearly we are convinc'd of this, when we least expect it, Providence appears the more in the Case, and our Security is shaken the more, and the more we are mov'd and terrified" (1:230). Religion not only heightens terror and wonder or admiration; it ennobles such base passions as grief.

Three things ultimately contribute to the perfection of poetry and therefore of tragedy: nature (or genius or passion), art ("those Rules, and that Method, which capacitate us to manage every thing with the utmost Dexterity, that may contribute to the raising of Passion"), and the richness of the language (1:245-46). Greek tragedy, Dennis says, was great because the Greek language was perfected, the art of poetry—particularly the art of tragedy—had been cultivated, and religion moved the passions of the people.

The ends of poetry and of true religion, or Christianity, are the same, Dennis states, although poetry falls short of religion, as human invention does of divine wisdom. Poetry contributes to a harmony between reason and passion, thus helping us to act freely and virtuously. Religious experience, particularly that of Christianity, has the same effect. Philosophers, on the other hand, reconcile the conflict between reason and passion by making either reason or passion supreme. Each of these alternative solutions of the philosophers fails, says Dennis. The poets, however, ''appear'd to have a Glimmering of the Truth'' (1:255). To attempt to repress or to moderate the passions, Dennis believes, establishes a psychological conflict in man, for the passions were unrestrained in man's original state, before the fall of Adam. Man ''can no more take away Love and Desire by Reasoning, than he can satisfy Hunger and Thirst with a Syllogism'' (1:258-59). This is the limitation of the Stoic and the deist, according to Dennis.

Love and desire must be made compatible with reason and order. Poetry and Christianity contribute to this end—the first through form or design, and the second, through faith in an ultimate justice governing human existence.

Christianity reconciles reason and passion by directing passion toward love of God and of one's neighbor. Poetry as an art satisfies the reason, the passions, and the senses, thus moving us toward virtuous action. Poetry also transmutes what is painful to us in life into an effect of pleasure, partly because we are secure in our realization that there is a difference between the experience of what is represented in art and the experience of actual living:

> Passions which plague and torment us in Life, please us, nay, transport us in Poetry . . . . For, tho' sometimes a vigorous lively Imitation of Creatures that are in their Natures noxious, may be capable of giving us Terror yet Nature, by giving us a secret Intelligence that the Object is not real, can turn even that tormenting Passion to Pleasure . . . . Poetry seems to be a noble Attempt of Nature, by which it endeavours to exalt itself to its happy primitive State; and he who is entertained with an accomplish'd Poem, is, for a Time, at least, restored to Paradise. That happy Man converses boldly with Immortal Beings. Transported, he beholds the Gods ascending and descending, and every Passion, in its Turn, is charm'd, while his Reason is supremely satisfied. Perpetual Harmony attends his Ear, his Eye perpetual Pleasure. Ten thousand different Objects he surveys, and the most dreadful please him. Tygers and Lions he beholds, like the first Man, with Joy, because, like him, he sees them without Danger. (1:264-65)

The concept of genius introduces into Dennis's critical theory an idea that allows him to respond to Shakespeare in a way that

Rymer could not. *An Essay on the Genius and Writings of Shakespeare* (1712) praises Shakespeare as "one of the Greatest Genius's that the World e'er saw for the Tragick Stage" (2:4). His beauties were his own; his defects the result of his education and the age in which he lived. He also wrote under the pressure of theatrical deadlines, and could not wait until such time as his spirits were warm and volatile. Though unfamiliar with the ancients and with the rules, "he had a natural Discretion which never cou'd have been taught him, and his Judgment was strong and penetrating" (2:4). He seemed to lack only leisure to discover the rules, of which he appeared so ignorant. Dennis pays tribute to Shakespeare's innate ability. He greatly admired Shakespeare's characterization—its justness, exactness, vividness—although he criticized his anachronisms, his failure to maintain unity of action in his historical plays, and his omission of poetic justice and a moral in some of his best tragedies. The violation of time and place, Dennis realized, was necessary for greater effect.

Shakespeare had an extraordinary talent for arousing the passions, especially terror, and his representation of them was so just, lively, and appropriate that he touches us more than other tragic poets, whose plotting and beauty of design are superior. Shakespeare's diction, in many places, is good and pure after a hundred years; his expression is "simple tho' elevated, graceful tho' bold, and easie tho' strong" (2:4). He seems, says Dennis, to have originated English tragic harmony—the harmony of blank verse, diversified by dissyllabic and trisyllabic endings. This diversity distinguishes it from heroic harmony, and brings poetic expression nearer to popular usage. It gains more attention, and is better fitted for action and dialogue than heroic verse.

Shakespeare, Dennis thought, had a genius for tragedy. If he had had the art of Sophocles and Euripides, he would have surpassed them. Though he admired the French, Dennis believed, as did Dryden, that many elements in the work of Shakespeare were greater. If he had been familiar with the Greeks, he would have imitated Sophocles and Euripides instead of Plautus, whose work, Dennis believed, Shakespeare had probably read in translation.

Shakespeare's lack of learning and art caused him, according to Dennis, to make serious mistakes in characters drawn from history and in the consistency and appropriateness of his characters. Because he did not know the rules, he made his incidents less moving, less surprising, and less wonderful than they might have been. Dennis, illustrating by reference to *Coriolanus*, says that Shakespeare seems almost industriously to have avoided taking advantage of the emotional effects in tragedy that compliance with the rules makes possible. On this point, Dennis was more right than he realized. Shakespeare broke the rules, if he was conscious of them, because he realized that if the artist is to advance he must go beyond established norms. They are useful as a basis of design but stagnating when followed undeviatingly.

Noting the absence of fable in Shakespeare's historical plays, Dennis states that the dramatist, in contrast to the historian, must select the episodes in history that contribute to a unified, dramatic action. History does not present, he says, the causes of events, as fiction does. Therefore, a fable, the fictional representation of a universal truth, is more appealing to the emotions of the audience than the representation of the particular truths of history. A series of historical episodes produces a confused emotional response in the audience rather than a pertinent and climactic one. Dennis realized that tragedy is a more moving experience for most of us than history, because it both universalizes and epitomizes history, and thus renders it meaningful. He did not see that Shakespeare started from the background of the mystery-play, the *Mirror for Magistrates,* and John Bale's *King John* to show history, and then realized that history provides a source for tragedy, because, as Aristotle knew, history is one kind of record of action having consequences, tragedy another kind.

Coriolanus, a play altered by Dennis to accord with his own theories, lacks, he believes, a moral, and most of Shakespeare's best tragedies violate poetic justice. As a man of his time, Dennis failed to realize what Shakespeare, no doubt, perceived—that the disproportionate consequence of the hero's action is precisely what makes his fate tragic, and that the nature of reality makes his fate what it is.

Shakespeare, concludes Dennis, was a genius who would have succeeded even better with a knowledge of the Greeks and of the rules; nonetheless, he ''had none to imitate, and is himself inimitable'' (2:4).

Although Dennis, as we shall see, is in many ways a neoclassical critic, the concept of genius makes his critical theory freer and more viable than Rymer's. The Longinian approach to literature views literature as process, the Aristotelian as product. Shakespeare in his tragedies is always developing—breaking his own molds. Ecstasis, or ''a state of identification in which the reader, the poem, and sometimes, at least ideally, the poet also, are involved,'' is basic to the approach of Longinus.[6] Aesthetic distance is more characteristic of Aristotle. Shakespeare, however, cannot be judged in terms of Aristotelian categories, first, because his tragedy stems partly from the conventions of earlier English drama, and, second, because he changed his style and form as his knowledge deepened, as his mastery of dramatic expression developed, and as popular taste in theatrical entertainment altered. Shakespeare's art is the art of process.

Dennis admits that good sense may be valuable in recognizing the immediately obvious qualities of a literary work, but he insists that the highest function of criticism, the ability to discern the ''beauties,'' or the nonstructural, less rational elements of a poetic work, requires genius. The critic, according to Dennis,

6. Northrop Frye, *Anatomy of Criticism* (Princeton, N.J.: Princeton University Press, 1957), p. 67.

must be a man with a strong and lively imagination tempered by sound judgment and experience of life. Referring in *The Impartial Critic* (1693) to Rymer's carping condemnation of Shakespeare and his unrestricted praise of Edmund Waller, Dennis remarks that a man who overlooks Waller's faults must also be capable of ignoring Shakespeare's excellencies: "For it is much more easie to find Faults, than to discern Beauties. To do the first requires but common Sence, but to do the last a Man must have Genius" (1:13).

Although Dennis believes that poetry should imitate nature, meaning what Louis I. Bredvold has called *"la belle nature,"* and should be related to the ancient classics, he values originality most of all. Shakespeare's glory, he says, was derived from the fact that his magnificent achievements were "entirely his own, and owing to the Force of his own Nature" (2:4).[7] Dennis attempts to reconcile originality with tradition, genius with the rules, passion with reason. Longinian ardor, vehemence, and elevation—qualities that induce agitation, rapture, and transport—are to be brought under the rational control associated with French neoclassicism. Arguing that adherence to the rules helps to insure the classical qualities of symmetry, proportion, and harmony, he supports them as reflections of a rational order governing the universe. At creation man had been in harmony with this order, but, through transgression, particularly through the conflict between reason and passion, man lost this original unity of intellect and feeling.

The function of poetry and of all the arts, Dennis believes, is to help restore man's inner harmony. The rules are a means to this end. They are based upon the example of great works, tested by the response of successive generations of men, and are therefore empirical and scientific. Homer and Virgil, states Dennis in *The Advancement and Reformation of Modern Poetry,* realized the

---

7. "Platonison in Neo-Classical Esthetics," ELH 1 (1934): 97ff.

necessity of following the rules, and they did not appeal to a narrow audience of fellow countrymen but "to their Fellow-Citizens of the Universe, to all Countries, and to all Ages" (1:203). The great classic writers were not without passion and imagination, yet they realized that nothing except what is great in reason and nature, meaning what reflects the harmonious order of the universe, can lastingly please mankind. The rules of poetry, like the rules of life and philosophy, are chiefly condemned, Dennis says, by those who either cannot understand them or cannot endure the labor of following them. As he states later in *The Causes of the Decay and Defects of Dramatic Poetry, and of the Degeneracy of the Public Taste* (1725?), when he has generally become more conservative: "if Poetry is not an Art, tis a meer whimsey and Fanaticism. If tis an Art it must have a System of rules, as evry art has, and that System must be known" (2:283).

The rules, according to Dennis, reflect the regularity of nature. Nothing in nature is beautiful without rule and order. The more rule and order in objects, the more they please our senses. The same is true in art, particularly in poetry: "For Poetry being an imitation of Nature, any thing which is unnatural strikes at the very Root and Being of it and ought to be avoided like Ruine" (1:40). Dennis draws an analogy between the order of creation reflected in nature and the order of man reflected in reason. "For Reason is Order, and the Result of Order.... Whatever God created, he designed it Regular" (1:202). Poetry can never swerve from the laws prescribed for it by reason. The more irregular a poem or tragedy is, the nearer it comes to extravagance, confusion, and nonsense. For example, Dennis finds Sophocles' *Oedipus Rex* more moving than Shakespeare's *Julius Caesar* because Sophocles' tragedy is just and regular, Shakespeare's extravagant and irregular (1:200). The English, says Dennis, are habituated to irregularity. They have clung to their gothic and barbarous style, whereas the French have recognized the need for rules. As a result French genius has blossomed, but the English stage has fallen from the imitation of nature and from its greatness at the time of Shakespeare "in whose *Coriolanus* and *Cassius,* we see something of the Invincible Spirit of the *Romans*" (1:203).

Nevertheless, Dennis qualifies his insistence upon regularity in poetry, just as he stresses genius while at the same time defending the rules. Some irregularities exist "even in the wonderful Dispensations of the Supreme and Sovereign Reason, as the Oppression of the Good, and Flourishing of the Bad," yet these irregularities mysteriously fulfill the designs of Providence (1:202-3). In the same way, parts of a poem or tragedy may appear irregular, and yet be necessary to the whole design. In considering the work as a whole, Dennis is faithful to Aristotle. He anticipates Coleridge in realizing the complex relationship of the parts of a poem to the total effect.

Dennis's attitude toward the rules partly reflects the prevalent rationalism of the age, but his ideas on the relation of genius to the rules and his appraisal of the function of passion in poetry are at a variance with the prevailing neoclassical temper. Aristotle's principles must be respected, Dennis believes, but a poet's devotion to the rules is no substitute for genius. Paul Spencer Wood considered Dennis in this respect one of "the Whigs of criticism," along with such figures as Sir Robert Howard, Samuel Butler, and William Temple. They wished to oppose abject servitude to the rules but not to overthrow Aristotelian principles.[8] Even in later years, when he more fully accepted neoclassical standards, Dennis recognized that sometimes greater effects can be obtained by ignoring the rules. However, he felt that in general beauty is best achieved through regularity. For this reason E.N. Hooker identified Dennis not as a precursor of Romanticism but as a responsible and intelligent classicist (2:xcix).

---

8. "The Opposition to Neo-Classicism in England between 1660 and 1700," *PMLA* 43 (1928): 196.

The rules, for Dennis, applied primarily to tragedy. In contrast to Dryden, who believed the epic to be the highest form of poetry, Dennis preferred tragedy. Tragedy, Dennis believes, must contain a fable, or fictionalized version of a universal truth, exemplified in a unified action, the characters of which are generally to be historical and significant. A fable, according to Dennis, "is a Discourse invented to form the Manners by Instructions disguised under the Allegory of an Action" (2:308). Dennis's view of tragedy reflects later seventeenth-century epic theory. It was generally thought that an epic poet began with a moral—an ethical, religious, or political precept, expressing the writer's general intention or plan, as Milton does at the beginning of *Paradise Lost*. Next, the poet constructed the fable or outline of a story to illustrate his precept.[9] The basic story or outline must be fictitious, general, and allegorical; the action represented a more concrete, restricted, and particularized working out of the fable; it involved the naming of characters and the fashioning of episodes. Aristotle believed that the poet should construct the plot of a tragedy before developing it in detail and that the plot should be original even if it contained traditional material. He did not connect the plot with a moral or give it an allegorical meaning. The characters in tragedy, Dennis maintains, must also be universal and allegorical. The purpose of the action is to prove the moral, and the action cannot be completed until the moral has been exhaustively worked out. Dennis criticized Dryden's *All for Love* because it lacked a moral and a fable, and, as noted previously, he objected to the lack of a fable in Shakespeare's historical plays.

The action of tragedy, according to Dennis, must have an allegorical or universal meaning capable of instructing the audience in moral conduct by arousing and purging the emotions of pity and fear in such a way as to bring the passions into harmony

---

9. Rymer, Dennis, and Dryden use the term *fable* with various meanings. *Fable* for Rymer meant plot; for Dryden, design; for Dennis, the general outline of the story that would illustrate the moral. See Dennis, 1:456 n.

with reason. The experience of tragedy, Dennis maintains, provides the emotional means to lead men to seek reasonable choices supported by the passions in harmony with the will. Witnessing a tragedy, he thought, should encourage virtuous living based on a union of rational conviction, passion, and desire. Dennis combines a fabulist and affective approach to the problem of tragic catharsis. The purgation of pity and fear contributes to moral utility.

Although Dennis occasionally develops decorum of manners as stolidly as Rymer did, he realizes that characters in tragedy cannot always reflect the ideal. He permits representation of evil characters in tragedy, provided they are shown to be what they are. Dennis acknowledges human uniqueness. A character's speech, however, he maintains, must accord with his rank and with propriety.

By reference to Horace, Freeman, the dialogist in *The Impartial Critic* who reflects Dennis's own thinking, explains, *"A Tragedy is Fabula recte morata,* in which the Manners are well painted: So that every Actor discovers immediately by what he says, his Inclinations, his Designs, and the very Bottom of his Character"* (1:35). Manners of epic characters, Dennis explains in *Remarks upon "Prince Arthur,"* following Le Bossu, should be *good* [well-delineated], *like* [in accord with tradition], *convenient* [appropriate], and *equal* [consistent]. In general, Dennis applies the same requirements to tragic characters. However, Dennis, in contrast to Rymer, notes that Aristotle permits the imitation of what is irregular in nature, but in this case the dramatist must make the incidents or character consistently unequal and irregular. Dennis not only follows Le Bossu's insistence that manners be well marked—with the hero's manners showing a predominant quality—but he also agrees with Le Bossu that characters should be delineated with varying degrees of intensity in proportion to their significance in the action.

Since the first purpose assigned to tragedy by Dennis in *The Impartial Critic* is to arouse and to purge the emotions of pity and terror, and the second—contrary to Aristotle—is through the fable to convey a moral lesson, the hero, according to Dennis, cannot be either an excessively virtuous one or one who is vicious. To bring a good man to misery would move neither compassion nor terror, but rather horror. An evil man brought to misery would arouse pleasure, but not horror or pity, "for terrour is caused in us by a view of the Calamities of our Equals; that is, of those who resembling us in their faults, make us, by seeing their Sufferings, apprehensive of the like Misfortune." The hero must be one "who keeping the middle between these extremes, is afflicted with some terrible calamity, for some involuntary fault" (1:19).

On the authority of Dacier's interpretation of Aristotle, Dennis explains that involuntary faults are not only those caused by invincible ignorance but those faults to which we are strongly inclined "either by the bent of our Constitution, or by the force of prevailing Passions" (1:20). By Aristotelian standards, Dryden's Oedipus is too virtuous, whereas the character of Sophocles' Oedipus, according to Dennis, is superbly suited to arouse compassion and terror, because the audience can readily see its own frailties and passions in those of the hero. (Dennis follows Dacier in placing even the source of pity in self-love.) The human weaknesses of Sophocles' hero alert the spectators to the fact that they themselves are capable of being driven by like passions to similar, if not identical, crimes. The spectators, it may be assumed, cannot identify themselves with a hero who demonstrates none of the unruly passions common to all men. Theoretically, then, Dryden's representation of Oedipus as a supremely virtuous man brought to a downfall should not arouse pity but horror, a murmuring against Providence, and consequently should fail to arouse terror. Since in fact Dryden's hero does arouse pity, says

Dennis, it is not completely true that the fall of the virtuous stirs
no compassion, but the emotion is not so intense as that aroused
by the sufferings "of those, who having some Faults, do the
more resemble ourselves" (1:21). Dryden's mistake in the conception of his tragic hero (a mistake also made by Corneille)
perpetrated by a lesser playwright would have been disastrous.
Dryden's powers as a dramatist, says Dennis, save the play. That
Aristotle would condemn the play or rescind his principles is
obvious, Dennis claims, but he would "love the Criminal"
(1:22). Aristotle would crown the poet before he would damn the
play. Dennis acknowledges Dryden's gifts as a dramatist, in spite
of the fact that he recognizes that Dryden's tragic hero is not
Aristotelian.

Addison's Cato, a Stoic, says Dennis in *Remarks upon Cato*
(1713), is another unsuitable tragic hero, not because he is without passion but because his whole bent is toward subduing his
feelings. He is too virtuous a character for tragedy. The other
characters in Addison's play are not proper to tragedy, says
Dennis. Their manners are poorly portrayed, inappropriate, and
inconsistent. Furthermore, the passions revealed in the play are
not tragic, and sometimes they are false. In *The Impartial Critic*,
Dennis defended love as a suitable subject for tragedy, but he
claims that love in *Cato* is not a tragic passion. Passions in
tragedy, according to Dennis, ought to result primarily from the
force of the incidents, not from the characters' weaknesses.
Dennis is Aristotelian in making action or plot rather than character
central in tragedy. The characters in *Cato* are all philosophers,
claims Dennis, whereas those in Otway's *The Orphan,* a tragedy
by which Dennis believes Addison had been influenced, correspond with Aristotle's requirements. The calamities of Otway's
characters are caused by involuntary faults occasioned by out-
rageous passion.

Dennis accepts the principle of probability, although not in the
same way as the more rigid Aristotelian formalists understood it.

In *Remarks upon "Prince Arthur,"* Dennis states that the episodes in an epic must be necessary and appropriate parts of the action, as indicated by Le Bossu. They must be supported by probable circumstances and have strict connection with other parts of the work, as the limbs of one body. The connection must not be verbal but "proceed from the necessity of the Action, or from the Probability of its Circumstances" (1:62). Dennis, however, allows more for Aristotle's "plausible impossibilities." Probability, he realizes, is complex, and servile adherence to the unities of time and place in tragedy, for example, can violate probability. Dennis believed in intelligent observance of the unities, but in his criticism of *Cato* he illustrates first the faults in Addison's play that result from not observing the rules and subsequently the errors that ensue from too precisely observing them. The unities of time and place "are mechanick Rules," which, if judiciously used, contribute to "the reasonableness of the Incidents," heighten probability, and contribute to the effectiveness of the dramatic "Deceit" (2:68). Badly used, they have precisely the opposite effect. No incident, says Dennis, on the authority of Aristotle, in a tragedy should be unreasonable. Dennis points out by means of textual criticism the absurdities of conduct and sentiment in relation to time and place in *Cato*.

Although Aristotle said nothing about unity of place, says Dennis, he implied it by making the chorus a helpful part of tragedy. Dennis defends unity of place if it does not conflict with the probability of the incidents in the play. Otherwise, he believes that it is best to ignore this convention.

Strict regularity, Dennis believed, demanded continuity of scenes, but this convention he regarded as one of the less important rules that might be broken if not in accord with the work as a whole.

Dennis upholds the principle of poetic justice, ascribing its popularity to Rymer. We do not really know men, says Dennis, or what they actually suffer. The creator of tragedy, however, can know his creation; he can know the extent of the characters' guilt and what they ought to suffer, and he is obliged to make this guilt and retribution manifest to his audience. "The Creatures of a poetical Creator have no Dissimulation and no Reserve. We see their Passions in all their Height, and in all their Deformity; and when they are unfortunate, we are never to seek for the Cause" (2:20). Even though the distribution of happiness and affliction is unequal in actual life, nonetheless, because man has an immortal soul, states Dennis, he may be justly rewarded after death. A fable, on the other hand, is only transitory; therefore, offenders in fable must be punished during the representation. Poetic justice, Dennis acknowledges, however, is a very imperfect imitation of God's justice.

Dryden's influence on Dennis is perceptible in *The Impartial Critic* (1693), an early work consisting of an introductory letter and five dialogues between two characters, Beaumont and Jack Freeman, in which Dennis attacks the use of the chorus as unsuited to the English stage. Dryden in *Heads of an Answer to Rymer* defended the Elizabethan dramatists by saying that the content and method of a literary work must suit the age and country for which it is written.[10] In *The Impartial Critic,* Dennis declares that love, a theme suited to the English climate and temperament, though not treated in Greek tragedy, is nonetheless a proper subject for English tragedy. (Love as a subject for tragedy, although opposed by Dacier, was supported by some French critics because it was considered to be the one most apt to

---

10. In 1677 or 1678 Dryden sketched *Heads of an Answer to Rymer,* found on the end pages of his copy of Rymer's *The Tragedies of the Last Age.* See F. G. Walcott, "John Dryden's Answer to Thomas Rymer's *The Tragedies of the Last Age,*" PQ, 15 (April 1936): 194-214. The work was not published in Dryden's lifetime. It was first published by Jacob Tonson in the 1711 edition of *The Works of Beaumont and Fletcher,* and later with the paragraphs rearranged by Samuel Johnson in the "Life of Dryden" in *Lives of the English Poets.* Dryden's copy of Rymer's book was subsequently burned. These texts and one printed by Saintsbury are all that are extant. See *Critical Works of Thomas Rymer,* p. xxxiv. See Also James M. Osborn. *John Dryden; Some Biographical Facts and Problems,* rev. ed. (Gainesville, Fla.: University of Florida Press, 1965), pp. 283-84.

stir pity.) Dennis's early defense of love as a theme appropriate for the English stage (a view he later repudiated) is an idea also expressed by Dryden in his unpublished notes. H. G. Paul's study, *John Dennis, His Life and Criticism,* suggests that the two men may have discussed literary problems, and that Dryden may have led Dennis to study the French critics.[11]

The Impartial Critic, employing arguments based on Dacier, is intended to answer Rymer's claim of superiority for the ancient method of tragedy. It also aims to refute Rymer's attacks on Shakespeare. Dennis is not hostile to Rymer, but he dislikes Rymer's style and his habit of finding only faults in Shakespeare's plays. Dennis never executed his contemplated defense of Shakespeare alluded to at the close of *The Impartial Critic,* although in 1712 he published *An Essay on the Genius and Writings of Shakespeare,* to which reference has been made earlier. The dialogue method employed in *The Impartial Critic,* by its very nature, suggests a freer, more exploratory approach to criticism than that of Rymer.

Freeman, in *The Impartial Critic,* remarking on Rymer's *The Tragedies of the Last Age* and *A Short View of Tragedy,* finds more learning in the latter and more good sense in the former. Dennis dislikes the design, method, and style of *A Short View of Tragedy.* Besides defining the purpose of tragedy and the nature of the tragic hero according to Aristotle, modified by Horace, *The Impartial Critic* answers Rymer's arguments in favor of the chorus, although Dennis actually devotes himself more to Dacier's comments on it than to those of Rymer, who supported the chorus largely because it was characteristic of the most effective classical tragedies.

The chorus, says Dennis, was adapted to the religion and temper of the Greeks, but since it has no such connection with the English, and is contrary to nature and probability, it ought to be banished from the stage. The rules of Aristotle are to be respected, he states, but they must be appropriately adapted to the customs of the nation and the age in which we live. The success of the French plays employing the chorus, says Dennis, does not prove Rymer's argument in its favor. The French have returned to the use of the chorus, he believes, as a capitulation to convenience.

A fable, the soul of tragedy, can exist without the chorus, but not without the episode. Episode is defined by Dennis as ''all that was between the singing of the Chorus, which is all our Modern Tragedy'' (1:31). Dacier points to the fact, says Dennis, that the chorus, at first the foundation of tragedy, has become the least essential part of it. The chorus, argues Dennis, is not necessary to maintain unity of place. It was not used by the Greeks to indicate separate divisions of the play, as it was by the Romans. The chorus merely sang four times between the intervals of the episodes. The chorus is also unnecessary to excite and to purge the emotions of pity and terror. In fact, the chorus, he believes, dilutes the emotional effects of tragedy. Furthermore, the function of the chorus to provide moral comment and guidance is adequately fulfilled, he says, by the purgation that tragedy provides and by the fable. No danger of misinterpretation exists if a tragedy is written as it should be. Aristotle, he notes, speaks very little of the chorus, considering how large a part it played in Greek tragedy. Furthermore, since the chorus was related to the Greek religion, Aristotle could not be expected to condemn it. This same fact may also have been significant with Horace.

Dacier, says Dennis, ascribes the use of the chorus to the superstition of the Greeks. Singing and dancing were intimately connected with their religion. (Dacier was suggesting that the early form of the chorus, which sang and danced instead of being related to the action, might be abandoned. Dennis interprets Dacier's remarks for his own purposes of argument.)

Dacier does state, Dennis admits, that the chorus aids in creating "a wholesome delusion" (1:36ff.). Drama, Dacier says, is a public action and therefore cannot be unobserved. The chorus is consequently necessary for verisimilitude. It is easier for one thousand spectators to imagine themselves in an open space at Mycenae or Thebes than to imagine themselves in the king's cabinet, frequently the setting of French tragedy that did not employ the chorus. Nonetheless, despite Dacier's connection of the chorus with dramatic "delusion," Dennis cannot concede that verisimilitude accords with the singing and dancing of a chorus to accompany suffering. Nor is it necessary to sustain continuity or unity of action, as Dacier had argued. The action in contemporary drama, Dennis states, does not break every time the music plays between the acts. Even those who do not know this from reading Aristotle will realize that an action without an end is absurd. Dennis adds, "The Rules of *Aristotle* are nothing but Nature and Good Sence reduc'd to a Method" (1:39). Fiddles between the acts—a convention referred to by Rymer—may be ridiculous, Dennis admits, but absurdity in ornament is preferable to absurdity in essentials. Dennis interprets Aristotle's remarks on the chorus much more accurately than Rymer, who makes it the essential part of tragedy. In fact, Dennis's whole theory of tragedy is closer in spirit to Aristotle's than is Rymer's. However, although Dennis's conception of the tragic hero, of unity of action, and of the primary importance of plot are Aristotelian, his ideas on allegory, moral utility, and poetic justice show the effects of French formalist criticism. Dennis is more liberal than Rymer in regard to probability. The wonderful, the "consistently inconsistent," and even the irregular are permitted in tragedy if they demonstrate an ultimate regularity. Both critics are somewhat casual about the unities of time and place. Dennis's appreciation of genius allows him to give greater weight to the total effect of tragedy than Rymer can according to his standards of common sense and the rules. Responsive to the grandeur, passion, and unity of Greek tragedy, Dennis is restricted by his belief in moral utility and poetic justice. Both critics' understanding of Aristotle is distorted by French interpretations.

Dennis's importance lies particularly in his consideration of the psychology of the artist. Furthermore, the emphasis he gives to passion as a stimulus to poetic composition shows that, in opposition to the rationalism of his age, he sensed the role in literary creation of what is now termed the unconscious. In this respect, he exhibits an openminded and probing interest in creative processes, and employs with originality the psychology of Hobbes, who had a similar interest.

In the introduction to his *Critical Essays of the Seventeenth Century* (1:cii), Spingarn, who regards Dennis as the typical critic of his time, notes particularly his contribution in calling attention to the effect of climate upon the literary temper of a nation. Religion, government, and social circumstances, according to Dennis, also play a part. The critic, he insists, must understand the age for which a work is written.

Dennis's consideration of literature from the viewpoint of the artist and the audience, his analysis of conditions affecting literature, and his recognition of the effect of social and political influences on public response connect him to some degree with the school of taste, and distinguish him from the strict neoclassicists and from the rationalists. Saint-Évremond was conscious of the importance of climate and environment in relation to literature. He also acknowledged the soundness of Aristotle's rules, but he would not admit that they apply for all time.

Dennis, however, does not belong to the school of taste, although he does recognize in art an element of genius that can be felt rather than analyzed. Along with Rymer, he supports the major neoclassical standards of probability, verisimilitude, and decorum, because he feels that they have been tested by time and human experience, but his interpretation of them is more relaxed and flexible than Rymer's. He believes in a reasonable, though not servile, imitation of the ancients, but in spirit he is with the moderns, who can equal the Greeks in tragedy, he maintains, if they will use Christianity as the Greeks used their religion.

Dennis's connection of tragedy with religion may too easily appear to be a confusion of the end of rhetoric, to persuade, or the end of propaganda, to convert, with the autonomous end of imitation. This is not true, however, for Dennis had some perception of the contribution of religion to myth and consequently to tragedy. The basic problem in Dennis's theory of tragedy is the same one that appears in Rymer's criticism. How can the rationalistic, providential view of the universe prevalent in the late seventeenth century be made compatible with the ultimately inexplicable fate of the tragic hero, who unknowingly violates the laws of reality, and as a result must suffer and frequently struggle not only to know himself but to know his fellowmen and the will of the gods? How can his suffering be presented in terms of moral utility and poetic justice? If Dennis had seen as clearly as the Greeks did that man must pay for his ignorance and that the gods must triumph, he would have realized that although we can trace the course of human tragedy we cannot fathom it. Above all, we cannot simplify it, as the upholders of moral utility and poetic justice must do. Myth and religion, both in some way residues of the unconscious wisdom of the race, at least serve to give us a feeling of meaning, and thus contribute to the cohesive unity essential to the tragic vision. Without such a controlling element, our response to tragedy might indeed be frenzied and despairing. Northrop Frye has noted the emancipating effect on the imaginative mind of "the transcendental and apocalyptic perspective of religion."[12] It was this perspective that Dennis was seeking.

Despite his loyalty to the norms of neoclassicism, Dennis defends the necessity for originality. In contrast to the rationalists

---

12. Frye, p. 125.

and the neoclassicists, he establishes genius as the ultimate standard by which he judges both poet and critic. His sympathetic treatment of the imagination and the passions predicts some of the changes that emerge in Romantic criticism, notably in that of Wordsworth and Coleridge. His praise of Shakespeare also attests to a shift from rigid, rationalistic criticism, particularly of the type exemplified by Rymer, to one of appreciative response.

Dennis's conservatism prevented him from developing his own insights as fully as he might have. His dependence upon *a priori* reasoning is unfortunately less stimulating and less convincing than Dryden's inductive, Socratic method of criticism, but there is no doubt that in contrast to Rymer, and even to Dryden, Dennis realized the pivotal function of passion—or the unconscious—in poetic creativity, and he insisted upon his conviction in forceful terms. In many ways his views suggest twentieth-century explanations of intuitive thinking so basic to an understanding of the poetic process: Not the graceful stylist that Dryden was, Dennis was eventually eclipsed by his more gifted contemporary.

4

John Dryden's Theory of Tragedy: "They, Who Have Best Succeeded on the Stage, Have Still Conform'd Their Genius to Their Age."

In contrast with Dennis, who is primarily interested in the source of genius, Dryden applies himself most particularly to the demands of the work itself and to its effects upon the audience in terms of the age in which he lived. Dryden has been variously regarded as a critic who vacillated between French Aristotelianism and English freedom, as a counterpart of Corneille, as a Socratic skeptic, as a supporter of the rules, and as a thinker who attempted above all to establish dramatic standards appropriate for his own time.

T. S. Eliot believed that Dryden's theory was "a compromise between Aristotle, as he understood Aristotle through distorting French lenses, and his own practice which is itself a compromise between earlier English practice and French practice." Much for which Dryden appeals to authority, Eliot believed, actually resulted from his own sense of structure operating against the formlessness of the English stage. Although he did not attribute to Dryden a sense of tragedy, considering him an "observer" rather than a creator, he did acclaim him the "first master of English criticism."[1]

Dryden's method of concrete and specific analysis in his discussion of Ben Jonson's *The Silent Woman* bears some similarity to that of Corneille, who in his three *Discours* and three *Examens* of his own tragedies realized the need for historical perspective in regard to Aristotle's *Poetics*. Dryden's outlook is usually wider, however, than Corneille's. As Pierre Legouis remarks, "Corneille gives us the theory of his own plays; Dryden not seldom rises to an appreciation of the works of other and greater playwrights than himself, including Corneille."[2]

Louis I. Bredvold maintains that the center of Dryden's thinking was philosophical skepticism. "It was a philosophical doubt, a dissolvent of dogmatism and fanaticism, which at its best induced in its adherents the virtues of intellectual humility and tolerance."[3] An exploratory cast of mind led Dryden to examine with care many sides of a question and to use the dialogue form in *An Essay of Dramatic Poesy*. This way of thinking also accounts for inconsistency in Dryden's opinions. He kept considering different views on literary questions, as he did on questions of religion and politics, and although skepticism drove him, as it did Montaigne, to religious and political conservatism, it did not move him to critical conformity.

Dryden's criticism exhibits a lively perception, an open-minded, tentative approach, and a clear, fluid manner of expression. Samuel Johnson speaks of the "elegance" of Dryden's style and the "thorns and brambles" of Rymer's. "Dryden's criticism," says Johnson, "has the majesty of a queen; Rymer's

1. *John Dryden: The Poet, the Dramatist, the Critic* (New York: T. & Elsa Holliday, 1932), pp. 58, 50-51.
2.   "Corneille and Dryden as Dramatic Critics," *Seventeenth Century Studies Presented to Sir Herbert Grierson* (Oxford: Clarendon Press, 1938), p. 282.
3.   *The Best of Dryden*, ed. Louis I. Bredvold (New York: Ronald Press, 1933), p. xxvii.

has the ferocity of a tyrant."[4] Dryden's tolerant consideration of various aspects of the dramatic art prevents him from succumbing to an *idée fixe*, as Rymer did. He avoided building his theories into a complete system. "For many a fair precept in poetry is," he wrote, "like a seeming demonstration in the mathematics, very specious in the diagram, but failing in the mechanic operation" (1:252).[5] Because his criticism, particularly in his prefaces and prologues, expresses his views in relation to the plays he was writing, his ideas change in the light of his practical experience.

Dryden occasionally remarks directly on the function and attitudes of the critic. He does not believe that the principal business of criticism is to find fault. He argues that criticism, an art first instituted by Aristotle, aims to establish standards for judging well and for noting "those excellencies which should delight a reasonable reader" (1:179). The judgment should be favorable, says Dryden, "if the design, the conduct, the thoughts, and the expressions of a poem, be generally such as proceed from a true genius of Poetry" (1:179). He refers sympathetically to Longinus's praise of sublime, yet erring, genius above mediocre, yet flawless, competency.

With Rymer as a target, Dryden makes a sharp comment on unsuccessful poets who vent their frustration in criticism: "Thus the corruption of a poet is the generation of a critic" (2:2-3). Dryden thinks that the function of the critic is to encourage excellence in poetry, to illuminate for others what is difficult to understand, and generally to guard the poet from irresponsible attacks. He realizes, too, that criticism can become an avenue of self-exploitation for the critic instead of a means of encouraging high standards on the part of the poet and sound responses on the part of the audience.

---

4.   "Life of Dryden," *Lives of the English Poets*, intro. by Arthur Waugh, 2 vols. (London, New York: Oxford University Press, 1906), 1:289.
5.   Citations of Dryden's criticism are to *Essays of John Dryden*, ed. W. P. Ker, 2 vols. (New York: Russell & Russell, 1961).

Dryden shares Dennis's belief in the validity of genres: "the first inventors," such as Homer and Virgil in the epic, "of any art or science, provided they have brought it to perfection, are, in reason, to give laws to it; and, according to their model, all after-undertakers are to build" (1:271). He believes, as Dennis does, that the excellence of what has pleased the judicious throughout the ages has been attested to by the force of universal tradition. Referring to Horace's insistence that a poem must form an artistic unity, he says, "True judgment in Poetry, like that in Painting, takes a view of the whole together, whether it be good or not; and where the beauties are more than the faults, concludes for the poet against the little judge" (1:264). He thinks, as Dennis does, that the opinion of the poet in regard to poetry is preferable to that of other men. Mere admiration, however, is not a sufficient basis for critical judgment. A man must consciously understand the excellences of tragedy, says Dryden, if he is to be a critic rather than "a blind admirer" (1:196).

The "blind admirer" lacks understanding and discrimination. The true critic responds to poetry, but understands it, and is able to demonstrate his judgments by rational exposition. In the dedication of the *Aeneis* (1695), following the French critic, Jean Regnauld de Segrais (1624-1701), one of the circle of the Hôtel de Rambouillet and later a member of the French Academy, Dryden divides the reading public into those who have true judgment based upon understanding and grasp of critical principles—the smallest group—and those who either having no principles or having inadequate ones are deficient in ability for right judgment.[6]

Samuel Johnson in his "Life of Dryden" spoke of him as the first writer who taught the English to criticize by rule. According to Johnson, he established a foundation of critical standards and

---

6. See Hoyt Trowbridge, "The Place of Rules in Dryden's Criticism," *MP* 44 (November 1946): 87-88.

principles upon which others could build. Spingarn called attention to Dryden's logical reasoning and to his skeptical, open-minded, Socratic approach. Referring to Dryden's combination of freedom with respect for authority and to the urbanity of discussion and conversation in *An Essay of Dramatic Poesy,* he described the work as a brilliant application of French neoclassical principles to English literature.[7] Saintsbury stated that Dryden displayed a certain casualness toward the rules, regarding them as restrictions that were incompatible with a profound conception of poetry.[8] Hoyt Trowbridge refutes Saintsbury's judgment: "But Dryden's view was very different. To him delight was the end of poetry, the imitation of nature its most general and basic means; the more specific rules were simply less general means to the same end."[9] Dryden believed, according to Trowbridge, that the process of criticism involves rational analysis based on principles which, though not certain, are probable. Dryden's critical method, he maintains, is not essentially skeptical but one based on intelligible standards. The rules are tentative hypotheses, amenable to change and modification.

Answering his brother-in-law, Sir Robert Howard, who accused him of assessing poetry by rigid rules—mathematical rules—when it should be judged by the light of individual preferences, Dryden, in *A Defence of An Essay of Dramatic Poesy* (1668), denies that he has taken a dictatorial approach, for he does not find "that the character of a positive or self-conceited person" is apt to find a receptive audience in his age (1:125). *An Essay of Dramatic Poesy* was a dialogue, he says, among people of various opinions, all left doubtful for the purpose of having the readers come to their own conclusions. The dialogue was particu-

---

7. *Critical Essays of the Seventeenth Century,* 1908 ed. 3 vols. (Bloomington Ind: Indiana University Press, 1963), 1: lxxviii, lxiii.
8. *A History of Criticism and Literary Taste in Europe,* 2nd ed., 3 vols. (Edinburgh and London: William Blackwood and Sons, 1911), 2:388-89.
9. *MP* 44: 90.

larly directed to the attention of Lord Buckhurst, to whom the work was dedicated. The propositions relating to the method of better imitating nature in *An Essay of Dramatic Poesy,* Dryden further states, were not his own, nor were they presented as such. They were derived from the authority of Aristotle and Horace and from the rules and example of Ben Jonson and Corneille. Dryden concedes that certainty in criticism is unachievable, but he regards probability as a sufficient basis for defining the rules. Dryden's method of reasoning, Trowbridge maintains, owes less to the tradition of skeptical thinking than it does to Aristotle's distinction in the *Posterior Analytics* (1:xxxiii) between "science," which deals with what is demonstrable, and "dialectic," which deals with what is probable. Dialectic, according to Aristotle, though an inferior method of reasoning, is employed in conclusions that concern variable things. This distinction was maintained in the usual differentiation between science and opinion.

It follows that if nature is to be imitated, says Dryden in *A Defence of An Essay of Dramatic Poesy,* there must be rules for imitating rightly. However, as the divines agree that there is a God and that he ought to be worshiped, but disagree as to the manner, Dryden hesitates to proceed further to define the means by which nature ought to be imitated, beyond describing the opinions of the ancients and the moderns and some of his own.

A Defence of An Essay of Dramatic Poesy, Trowbridge believes, establishes three principles in regard to the function and status of the rules in criticism: taste cannot be the criterion of judgment; it is possible to establish rules on an objective basis and to support them reasonably; such principles are not completely demonstrable and therefore not dogmatic. Dryden's insistence that criticism requires some standard independent of opinion Trowbridge finds consistent throughout Dryden's work.

Robert Lathrop Sharp in his study *From Donne to Dryden* has commented on the tension existing in the later seventeenth century between respect for the classical tradition and fear of the stifling effect on poetry of too strict insistence on rules. Desire for experimentation, Sharp explains, existed simultaneously with a demand for precision about the principles of poetry. Because science was becoming increasingly exact, it was felt, why could not the art of poetry be similarly clarified? Dryden, for example, attempts to fix the approximate degree of freedom permitted in poetic metaphor—an effort at once understandable and yet impossible. Ben Jonson, says Sharp, believed in certain basic rules in poetry, but he did not try to explain every detail in regard to art: "By Dryden's time formalism had increased until rules were found for every step in the poetic process. Dryden was a moderate formalist in comparison with Rymer, but in comparison with Jonson he seems often unwisely insistent about rules and propriety."[10]

William E. Bohn's "The Development of Dryden's Literary Criticism," published in 1907, divides Dryden's work into five periods, corresponding to his favor or lack of favor at court. Before the close of 1665, according to Bohn, Dryden was independent and open-minded, expressing a love for the English language, although he voiced some desire to see it regulated by an authority such as the French Academy. He praised the romantic plays of Shakespeare, and defended neoclassical rhyme. This period includes *An Essay of Dramatic Poesy,* although it was not published until 1668.

From 1666 to 1675, Bohn claimed, Dryden retreated from his earlier innovations and devoted his criticism to the exploration and defense of the heroic ideal. His conception of poetry consequently became somewhat mechanical. He also attacked Elizabethan drama. The third period, from 1675 to 1679, marked for Bohn a return on the part of Dryden to the spirit of *An Essay of Dramatic Poesy.* Dryden again expressed his love for Shakes-

---

10. *From Donne to Dryden* (Chapel Hill, N.C.: University of North Carolina Press, 1940), p. 203.

peare and attempted to imitate him. The fourth period, from 1680 to 1689, corresponding as it did with Dryden's service at court, Bohn considered one of meager and coldly rationalistic criticism. In the fifth period, beginning with the reign of William and Mary, during which Dryden lost his government fees and pensions and became a full-time man of letters, he regained, according to Bohn, his moral and intellectual independence.[11]

The first, third, and fifth periods were, as Bohn saw them, ones of originality and freedom; the second and fourth, ones of conformity. Bohn's analysis of Dryden's criticism, although useful as a frame of reference for Dryden's thinking, connects the changes in his critical viewpoint too exclusively with his state of political security or insecurity.

Dryden's critical method may be described as that of an intelligent, practicing poet and playwright, aware of French critical theory, respectful of classical form and simplicity, but also appreciative of the vitality and psychological force of Shakespeare and the Elizabethan dramatists. Dryden is interested in how to write, in how an author has written, and in how to assess a writer's work.[12] His critical approach is not only inductive, analytical, and rational but also psychological. He attempts to arrive at principles in relation to literature by Socratic consideration of various possibilities. He tries to isolate the elements in the classical tradition, in French critical theory, and in the English theater of his own age and of the previous one that can be profitably combined into a new form. His innate responsiveness to what is authentically good allows Dryden to trust his sensibility and intuition, but as a critic he tries to explain his judgments on a rational basis. His skepticism keeps him open minded and allows him to be flexible—even inconsistent. Ultimately, however, it is

11. "The Development of John Dryden's Literary Criticism," *PMLA* 22, n.s. 15 (1907): 66-135.
12. David Nichol Smith, *John Dryden* (Cambridge: University Press, 1950), p. 18.

something beyond wide reading, clear analysis, and reference to the rules and standards of his own age that makes Dryden the critic he is. He simply "had one of the most superb critical instincts ever born into the world."[13]

Dryden's critical method is not rigid, as is Rymer's, nor does it demonstrate Dennis's preoccupation with the psychological origins of poetic composition, although Dryden is interested in creative processes. Dryden's rational, essentially practical, analysis of the principles of poetry and drama is intricate because he is aware that the subject is complex. He is not afraid to change his mind, although in literary matters he does not change it to the extent that Margaret Sherwood suggested when she argued that Dryden wavered between French rigidity and English latitude, basing his judgments sometimes on a rationalist approach and sometimes on intuition.[14]

Dryden subscribes to the concept of poetry as the imitation of nature, but he uses the term in various senses at different times. He recognizes if he does not resolve the problem of deciding what "to imitate nature" means in his age. Is it the imitation of the ancients? Of the Elizabethans? Does it mean literal verisimilitude, or dramatic "delusion," in the sense of something very close to actual deception? Is it the imitation of *"la belle nature"?* Or is it the direct imitation of "human nature, in its actions, passions, and traverses of fortune," in a universe more complicated and fragmented than that of Aristotle?

All the central ideas in Dryden's criticism concerning probability, characterization, verisimilitude, the unities, and the use of rhyme are connected with the problem of what to imitate nature means in his age. Do the ancients, the Elizabethans, the French, or the moderns imitate nature best? Dryden reveals the most

---

13.   John Harrington Smith, "Dryden's Critical Temper," *Washington University Studies, Humanistic Series,* 12 (April, 1925): 219.
14.   *Dryden's Dramatic Theory and Practice* (Boston, New York, London: Lamson, Wolffe and Co., 1898), pp. 28 ff.

perceptive and free use of the concept in his positive evaluations
of Shakespeare and of the Elizabethan dramatists or, when he is
under the influence of Longinus, in his defense of bold, figurative expression in poetry.

In the Epistle Dedicatory of *The Rival Ladies* (1664), describing the difficulties of dramatic composition, Dryden said:

> Plotting and writing in this kind are certainly more troublesome em-
> ployments than many which signify more, and are of greater moment
> in the world; the fancy, memory, and judgment, are then extended
> (like so many limbs) upon the rack; all of them reaching with their
> utmost stress at Nature; a thing so almost infinite and boundless, as
> can never fully be comprehended, but where the images of all things
> are always present. (1:3).

The reference to nature in this case is not mechanistic, nor is it,
on the other hand, limited to Aristotle's "men in action," nor to
mere emulation. Eugenius in *An Essay of Dramatic Poesy*
objects to Crites's disparagement of the moderns, saying that dull
imitation of the ancients would be futile, for, although the moderns owe much to the ancients, they have been able to advance
beyond them because their own insight into nature has been en-
riched by their knowledge of the past. "We draw not therefore
after their lines, but those of Nature," says Eugenius, and thus
reach new dimensions that the ancients missed (1:43-44). If science has advanced, suggests Eugenius, cannot poetry and the
other arts also initiate new beauties?

Dryden shows himself to be aware that scientific progress has
made nature more intricate than it was when Aristotle spoke of
nature, meaning primarily "human nature." Noting the advances
in optics, medicine, and anatomy, Crites calls attention to the fact
that advances in philosophy have revealed "almost a new Nature" (1:36). Eugenius, arguing for the contribution of the moderns, points out that the ancients had no regular division of plays
into acts, although he acknowledges that Aristotle's description
of the exposition, rising action, peripety, and catastrophe was the

basis of the later Horatian division into five acts. The ancients, he says, maintained *liaison des scènes* better than the moderns, but their characters were fewer, and they sometimes failed to follow their own rules, with the result that they misrepresented nature. Furthermore, they frequently violated poetic justice. The unity of place was not found in Aristotle or Horace, but was introduced by the French. The ancients also sometimes perpetrated absurdities in trying to observe the rules. Eugenius appears to approve of the unities, but at the same time suggests that they lack a basis in authority or aesthetic judgment. The range of passion in ancient tragedies, he notes, too, was narrow, love being omitted. Eugenius implies that progress in drama can be achieved by conscious mastery of craftsmanship directed by judgment.

Dryden, however, valued the quality of genius above everything else. Shakespeare, he knew, was a natural genius, "the man who of all modern, and perhaps ancient poets, had the largest and most comprehensive soul. All the images of Nature were still present to him, and he drew them, not laboriously, but luckily; when he describes any thing, you more than see it, you feel it too" (1:79-80). Shakespeare did not need to discover nature through books—"he looked inwards, and found her there" (1:79). Here *mimesis* as interpreted by Dryden in relation to Shakespeare is not limited to the imitation of external reality but includes inner reality expressed in the whole motion of a work as a whole. This interpretation captures the real meaning of Aristotle's theory. Dryden admires Ben Jonson, "the more correct poet," who observed the rules, but he loves Shakespeare, the genius who ignored them.

An Essay of Dramatic Poesy, a defense of the English writers against those who prefer the French, answers Sir Robert Howard's attack on rhyme, and presents different viewpoints on questions of form in drama by means of a dialogue carried on by four characters, Crites, Lisideius, Eugenius, and Neander, against the background of a naval battle between the Dutch and the English. Crites is usually identified with Sir Robert Howard, Lisideius with Sir Charles Sedley, Eugenius with Charles, Lord Buckhurst (later Earl of Dorset), and Neander with Dryden himself.[15] Neander speaks last, after arguments relating to the ancients versus the moderns, the French dramatic method versus the English, and the value of the unities have been presented by other speakers.

Lisideius defines a play as "*a just and lively image of human nature, representing its passions and humours, and the changes of fortune to which it is subject, for the delight and instruction of mankind*" (1:36). This definition in relation to tragedy shifts the emphasis from Aristotle's "actions of men," to "passions and humours," and adds a didactic purpose to tragedy, thus reflecting French formalist theory and the influence of the epic on tragedy. Dryden wavers in his criticism between stressing pleasure and stressing moral utility as the primary end of poetry.

The argument for the unities in *An Essay of Dramatic Poesy* comes close to equating imitation with literal verisimilitude and compliance with the rules. The ancients, says Crites, expressing a strict neoclassical position, were "faithful imitators and wise observers of that Nature which is so torn and ill represented in our plays; they have handed down to us a perfect resemblance of her; which we, like ill copiers, neglecting to look on, have rendered monstrous and disfigured" (1:38). All the rules of drama regarding plot, narration, and ornament are derived from Aristotle, says Crites, mentioning at the same time Horace's *Ars poetica* as an excellent commentary on Aristotle. From the work of these two men, he states, has been derived the theory of the three unities. (Eugenius later points out that the unity of place was not a rule in Aristotle, but was first made one by the French poets.)

---

15. George Saintsbury, *Dryden* (London and New York: Harper & Bros., 1930), p. 126. See George Williamson, "The Occasion of *An Essay of Dramatic Poesy*," *MP* 44 (August 1946): 1-9. Williamson believes that the connection of the work with Sir Robert Howard has been exaggerated, and associates it with an exchange between Samuel Sorbière and Thomas Sprat.

In his discussion of unity of place and of *liaison des scènes* as described by Corneille, Crites regards dramatic illusion as dramatic "delusion," an attempt to approximate literal verisimilitude. Samuel Johnson later said in his *Preface to Shakespeare* that no one is deceived into mistaking a dramatic representation for reality:

> The truth is, that the spectators are always in their senses, and know, from the first act to the last, that the stage is only a stage, and that the players are only players . . . . The lines relate to some action, and an action must be in some place, but the different actions that compleat a story may be in places very remote from each other; and where is the absurdity of allowing that space to represent first *Athens,* and then *Sicily,* which was always known to be neither *Sicily* nor *Athens,* but a modern theatre?

Anyone capable of the first exercise of imagination "may imagine more," says Johnson, dispensing with the unities of time and place. Louis I. Bredvold points out that we regard the rules as merely traditional and mechanical aids, whereas their formulators regarded them as essential to an imitation of nature that could rationally be accepted by the audience.[16]

In an attempt to escape the constrictions imposed on drama by the unities of time and place and yet retain verisimilitude, Dryden says in *A Defence of An Essay of Dramatic Poesy* that the stage can represent two imaginary places successively. He distinguishes between a real and an imaginary place: "the imagination of the audience, aided by the words of the poet, and painted scenes, may suppose the stage to be sometimes one place, sometimes another; now a garden, or wood, and immediately a camp"

---

16. "Platonism in Neo-Classical Esthetics," *ELH* 1 (1934): 92. A. W. Verrall showed that insistence upon the three unities resulted from an attempt to construct a theory of drama that would correspond to *"authorities misunderstood."* The fundamental error, he explains, arose from misinterpreting both "the nature of dramatic or other artistic representation" and "Aristotle's theory of dramatic representation." Nevertheless, even a strong imagination, he remarks, requires some "imitation of nature." Obviously, "there is a 'nature' for dragons; a dragon reasonably 'swinges the scaly horror of his folded tail'; a dragon should not hang out the wash upon drying lines." *Lectures on Dryden* (Cambridge: University Press, 1914), p. 133.

(1:127). Neither the ancients nor the moderns, says Dryden, believed that they could make one place two, but they could have believed that a change of scene "might lead the imagination to suppose the place altered" (1:127). Dryden acknowledges that a certain latitude must be allowed to the unity of place—places adjacent to one another may be encompassed under the general concept of one place, but "the nearer and fewer those imaginary places are, the greater resemblance they will have to truth; and reason, which cannot make them one, will be more easily led to suppose them so" (1:129).

Such an involved discussion of the unity of place strikes the modern mind an unnecessarily tedious, but for the practicing playwright, such as Dryden, dealing with an audience unaccustomed to the quick adjustments that can now be taken for granted, the problem was a real one.

The same difficulty arises in regard to the unity of time. Dryden believes that the imaginary time span of twenty-four hours can be more naturally represented than the passage of twenty-four years. As the proportion is smaller, the verisimilitude is greater: "The imaginary time of every play ought to be contrived into as narrow a compass, as the nature of the plot, the quality of the persons, and the variety of accidents will allow" (1:130). The time span in tragedy, according to this principle, will naturally be greater than in comedy. The thinness of the plots in French plays prevents the overloading of incidents to be imagined in a certain space of time, but few Englishmen, says Dryden, except Ben Jonson have made a plot the content of which seems naturally confined to twenty-four hours. In a choice between thinness of plot and crowding many incidents into a small compass of time, Dryden considers the latter the more pardonable fault. There are degrees of impossibility, says Dryden. He realized, as Corneille had, the practical and artistic problems facing the dramatist in respect to observing the unities, but the fashion of the age as well as his own desire for a tightly unified tragic action prevented him from totally rejecting these conventions.

T.S. Eliot believed that in regard to the question of the unities of time and place Dryden's views were sound. Eliot acknowledged his own interest in the unities and expressed the belief that they would be significant in the drama of the future: "For one thing, we want more concentration. All plays are now much too long.... The Unities do make for intensity, as does verse rhythm."[17]

The argument about rhyme in *An Essay of Dramatic Poesy* also reflects the problem of the meaning of imitation. Crites objects to Neander's conclusion that rhyme is suitable for the stage. He argues that rhyme is unnatural in a play. Dialogue should give the impression of sudden thought. Consequently, Aristotle recommended writing tragedy in the kind of verse nearest prose. In English, blank verse is "nearest nature" (1: 91). With rhyme "the hand of art will be too visible" (1:92). Even though we know it to be a play, "a play is still an imitation of Nature; we know we are to be deceived, and we desire to be so; but no man ever was deceived but with a probability of truth" (1: 92).

Neander maintains that although he does not object to blank verse in tragedy, nonetheless, in a drama in which the subject and characters are great and in which no comic element is introduced, rhyme is as natural as blank verse, and more effective. He proceeds to argue that skill can make rhyme as unobtrusive as blank verse.

If rhyme can be employed in the epic, what is the objection to its use in tragedy, asks Neander. Since tragedy deals with the fortunes of noble persons, "heroic rhyme is nearest Nature, as being the noblest kind of modern verse" (1:101). Crites had objected that verse does not present the effect of sudden thought, since the thoughts will be expressed in a way that would not be natural without premeditation. Neander replies, "A play ... to

---

17. "A Dialogue on Poetic Drama," *Of Dramatick Poesie, An Essay, 1668, by John Dryden; Preceded by A Dialogue on Poetic Drama by T.S. Eliot* (London: F. Etchells & H. Macdonald, 1928), p. xxvii.

be like Nature, is to be set above it; as statues which are placed on high are made greater than the life, that they may descend to the sight in their just proportion'' (1:102). Some latitude, says Neander, must be permitted the poet or he will be dismounted from his Pegasus and forced to follow nature on foot. Dryden is arguing that art depends upon conventions that must be understood and appreciated by both poet and audience; it must be in this sense an abstraction from life. Neander's argument shows Dryden's realization that the mimetic process entails creating speech that has some likeness to actual human speech but is at the same time different from actual speech. People in real life do not speak in blank verse or rhyme. Dialogue in drama is artfully created by the poet with the purpose of contributing to the movement of the work as a whole. The particular form the poet imposes on his language will depend in part upon what convention the audience is accustomed to or capable of comprehending. Shakespeare and Beaumont and Fletcher, Dryden recognizes, wrote to please the times in which they lived, but he said, ''the genius of every age is different'' (1:99). If the audience is overly conscious of the technique employed by the poet, ''the hand of art'' is too obvious. Dryden came to realize that rhyme in English is more prone to be obtrusive than blank verse. It is not so much a question of how the artist chooses to imitate outward or, more importantly, inward reality as it is a question of how convincing his method of imitation appears to be.

Through Lisideius in *An Essay of Dramatic Poesy* Dryden presents the standard views of the French neoclassicists. The French have been faithful to the ancients by scrupulously maintaining the unities of time, place, and action. Their plays have no underplots, in contrast to the disunity of English tragicomedy, a dramatic form that Lisideius vigorously attacks, saying that the mingling of mirth and compassion is incompatible with the purpose of tragedy. French tragedy has improved on the ancient models by its observance of poetic justice and its use of material from history as a basis for tragedy. In contrast to the English, the French are skillful in exposition, and careful to observe decorum. The English, on the other hand, with theatrical ineptness, present death on the stage.[18] Cruel or implausible actions, Lisideius argues, should be related as well as those intended to avoid tumult or to reduce the time compass, and those defective in beauty. Such practice was common with the ancients, he says, and continues to be with the best modern playwrights. The French also employ the *deus ex machina* ending less frequently than the English. Lisideius insists on the importance of *liaison des scènes*, and praises the use of rhyme in tragedy. Lisideius is concerned with means, Neander with ends. The presentation of the two viewpoints reflects an exchange between a spokesman for practice and a spokesman for theory.

Neander acknowledges the superiority of the French in regularity of plot, in fidelity to the laws of comedy and tragedy, and in decorum of the stage, but disagrees that they are generally superior. French drama, lacking humor and passion, is statuelike; its cold, declamatory style fails to arouse a strong response. Short speeches beget more "concernment" (1:72).

Neander defends tragicomedy, a form originated by the English, above any type of drama, ancient or modern. "He [Lisideius] tells us, we cannot so speedily recollect ourselves after a scene of great passion and concernment, as to pass to another of mirth and humour, and to enjoy it with any relish: but why should he imagine the soul of man more heavy than his senses?" (1:69). Comic elements, says Neander, provide the occasional, needed emotional relief, a function also performed by music between the acts. Neander is not convinced that passion and mirth destroy one another. He believes that it is to the honor

---

18.   David Daiches suggests that violence was more appropriate to the Elizabethan stage, where the setting was symbolic, than to the picture-frame stage of the Restoration. The ritualistic quality of Greek acting, he maintains, made convincing representation of violence impossible. *Critical Approaches to Literature* (Englewood Cliffs, N.J.: Prentice-Hall, Inc., 1956), p. 206.

of the English that they have invented, developed, and perfected this way of writing for the stage. Through Neander's comments, however, Dryden indicates that a mixture of tragic and comic scenes may be hazardous unless deliberately and skillfully handled. In having Neander describe the humorous parts of Elizabethan tragedy as comic relief, Dryden reveals the viewpoint of a practicing playwright assessing technique rather than that of a critic evaluating the complex quality of imitation involved. The comic parts of Shakespearean tragedy, for example, serve not only to alleviate the emotional tension of tragedy but to increase the many angles from which the core of the tragedy may be seen.

Neander attacks the French plots as barren in comparison to the variety and scope of the English. He also maintains that the greater number of characters in English plays adds to the interest of the plots. In this essay Dryden favors a dramatic unity that incorporates a well-ordered variety: "If then the parts are managed so regularly, that the beauty of the whole be kept entire, and that the variety become not a perplexed and confused mass of incidents, you will find it infinitely pleasing to be led in a labyrinth of design, where you see some of your way before you, yet discern not the end till you arrive at it" (1:73). He cites *The Maid's Tragedy, The Alchemist,* and *The Silent Woman* as examples of drama fulfilling this unity through variety. Suspense, excitement, and variety must be maintained in a play, Dryden believes, yet a steadily rising action and an increasing complication must move toward a climax and resolution. These were the standards of dramatic structure by which he criticized a play.

In considering the problem of decorum, Neander agrees that there is sound reason for not presenting violence on the stage, but, he objects, the English temperament and the tradition of the English stage lead the audience to expect some representation of this sort. He agrees both on the basis of Lisideius's argument and on the practice of Ben Jonson that death should not be shown on the stage. If the English are to be blamed for showing too much action on the stage, however, the French are to be criticized for showing too little. Too rigid adherence to the unities of time and place can also result in a thin plot and "narrowness of imagination" (1:76). Since English plays have greater variety of plot and livelier writing than those of the French, it is strange that plays in verse are criticized as imitations of the French:

> We have borrowed nothing from them; our plots are weaved in English looms: we endeavour therein to follow the variety and greatness of characters which are derived to us from Shakespeare and Fletcher; the copiousness and well-knitting of the intrigues we have from Johnson; and for the verse itself we have English precedents of elder date than any of Corneille's plays. (1:78).

Dryden was seeking to establish a mean between the constricting regularity of French tragedy and the undisciplined irregularity of the English. Claiming that many English plays are as regular as the French, Neander shows his preference for the irregular plays of Shakespeare and Fletcher, which display "a more masculine fancy and greater spirit in the writing" than those of the French (1:79). Dryden is consistent in his defense of the English dramatists in comparison both to the ancient Greeks and to the French. In the dedication of the *Examen Poeticum* or *Third Miscellany* (1693) he answers Rymer's attacks upon him and the Elizabethan dramatists by arguing that the English have moved beyond the "rudiments" of the Greek stage by dispensing with the unnecessary encumbrance of the chorus. Many tragedies of the former age surpassed, he claims, those of Sophocles and Euripides. The English, by demanding variety of episode, a subplot, and many actors, require a more difficult design in tragedy than the French, who are satisfied with narrow plots and fewer characters.

Dryden was anxious to discover what should be imitated in the drama of Shakespeare, Fletcher, and Jonson and what should be avoided. He wanted to establish standards to be founded on the analysis of significant models. *Defence of the Epilogue* or *An Essay on the Dramatic Poetry of the Last Age* (1672) makes a comparison between the Elizabethan age and his own on three points: language, wit, and conversation. Dryden expresses the opinion that the moderns excel the Elizabethans in grammatical propriety, and that they are also superior in plotting to Fletcher and Shakespeare but not to Jonson. Dryden in this essay is conscious simultaneously of the genius of Shakespeare and of his unevenness: "He is the very Janus of poets; he wears almost everywhere two faces; and you have scarce begun to admire the one, ere you despise the other" (1:172). Remarks such as this led Saintsbury to regard the essay as a deviation for Dryden, and Margaret Sherwood to see it as a reflection of his coming under French influence. Trowbridge maintains that the essay is not a general attack on the Elizabethans. He discounts any radical reversal from the opinions Dryden put forward in *An Essay of Dramatic Poesy*. Allowances must be made, he insists, for the dialogue form of the earlier essay and for the different purposes in the two works. Neander in *An Essay of Dramatic Poesy* admitted substantially the same faults in the plays of the Elizabethans that Dryden describes in the later essay. The negative criticism of Lisideius served to indicate the weaknesses of Shakespeare and Fletcher. The French plots, Lisideius noted, are more regular than the English; the laws of comedy and tragedy, as well as the decorum of the stage, are more strictly observed by the French. Neander praised the greatness and variety of characters in Shakespeare's plays, and drew attention to the effective representation of love and the wit in repartee in Beaumont and Fletcher's. These are practically identical excellences and faults, according to Trowbridge, that Dryden ascribes to the same poets in the later essay.[19]

---

19.   "Dryden's *Essay on the Dramatic Poetry of the Last Age*," *PQ* 22 (July 1943): 240-50.

As John Harrington Smith pointed out, Dryden's rationalism was the very quality that helped him as a critic of Shakespeare:

> It enabled him to see faults, without blinding him to virtues. It enabled him to maintain that sympathetic and yet detached attitude which the out-and-out romanticist will never attain. He does not prostrate himself before Shakespeare; neither does he search for his own soul in what Shakespeare writes. He approaches him as a great companion writer; with due respect but without undue reverence.[20]

Dryden moves in *An Essay of Dramatic Poesy* from his originally intricate view of imitation expressed in the Epistle Dedicatory of *The Rival Ladies* to a Socratic consideration of neoclassical standards, those of the French and of the moderns, concluding the essay with a tentative presentation of his own. At the time *An Essay of Dramatic Poesy* was written he supported a reasonable adherence to the unities and advocated the use of rhyme in tragedy. He was conscious, too, that as a result of intellectual and scientific progress, servile imitation of the ancients would mean deadness and regression, and was aware of the vitality of Elizabethan drama in comparison to the statuelike perfection of the French plays. Recognizing the psychological value of introducing comic scenes into tragedy, he referred to national differences affecting drama. He appreciated the unity achieved through variety and complexity in the design of romantic art, and, placing Shakespeare, the irregular dramatist, above Jonson, "the more correct," he was sensitive to the fact that the spirit of the time called for a new type of genius and new forms of drama, but he was unclear about what direction the genius of the age should take.

A Defence of An Essay of Dramatic Poesy asserted the Socratic purpose and method of Dryden's first essay, and refuted Howard's accusation against him of dogmatism. Acknowledging

---

20. "Dryden's Critical Temper," *Washington University Studies, Humanistic Series,* 12 (April 1925): 216.

a desire to please his audience and to adapt his genius to the demands of his own age, he defended the use of rhyme in serious plays and adherence to the unities of time and place. He also concerned himself with the problem of probability in drama, generally narrowing the concept, but conceding that there are degrees of probability.

In *An Essay on the Dramatic Poetry of the Last Age*, Dryden attempted to reach objective standards for the writing of plays and for the critical evaluation of them. He was trying to establish some critical hypotheses to guide himself as a dramatist and critic as well as to release criticism from domination by the vague, subjective criterion of taste.

In *A Parallel of Poetry and Painting* (1695), prefixed to his translation of Du Fresnoy's *De arte graphica*, Dryden, translating from Bellori's *Lives of the Painters*, considers the tradition that requires the artist to imitate the Platonic form rather than what he actually sees in nature. According to this view, because nature makes nothing perfect, it is inferior to art when art imitates the ideal. Dryden notes that just as this principle is of little use in the painting of portraits, so it is inapplicable to the characters of comedy and tragedy, because these characters cannot be perfect. They must be as they have been described in history, if real, or such as poets first represented them, if fictitious. The excellence of stage characters, says Dryden, depends on ''their likeness to the deficient faulty nature, which is their original'' (2:125). The better rather than the worse likeness is to be chosen, however, as the painter paints the side of the face without a blemish or shadows the imperfect side. Nevertheless, all imperfections of the characters must not be removed, for some basis of pity for their misfortunes has to be provided, especially in the case of the tragic hero.

In this work Dryden upholds the rules as the best guide to imitating nature. Poetry and painting give us an imitation not just of nature but ''of the best Nature, of that which is wrought up to a nobler pitch," more perfect than in any individual. As a consequence, we can delight "to see all the scattered beauties of Nature united by a happy chemistry, without its deformities or faults" (2:137). Both poetry and painting must especially imitate the passions, according to Dryden, for unless the passions are moved, there can be no delight. As do Dennis, Hobbes, and Descartes, Dryden identifies pleasure with the agitation of the passions.

There is no rule, however, for invention. "A happy genius is the gift of nature" (2:138). Invention involves the disposition of the work: "to put all things in a beautiful order and harmony, that the whole may be of a piece" (2:139). Although the customs and times of those represented must be imitated, the masters must also be followed, "who understood Nature better than we," for nature "is always the same, though in a different dress" (2:139). Adapting to poetry Du Fresnoy's ideas on design in painting, Dryden states that the characters in drama must be distinguished from one another, action and dialogue must be consistent with manners, and the tragic hero, who is the object of pity, must be in the foreground, with the minor characters or episodes arranged with appropriate perspective or proportion.

Dryden's view of nature as *"la belle nature"* is reflected in the heroic play, a dramatic form derived from the epic, a genre he considers superior to tragedy. Dryden says in the dedication of the *Aeneis* (1697), "Tragedy is the miniature of human life; and epic poem is the draught at length" (2:157). In 1672 he had defined a heroic play as "an imitation, in little, of an heroic poem," in which love and valor constitute the main themes (1:150). Everything in the play is to be heightened. Consequently, the language of poetry should not resemble too closely the language of ordinary conversation. Nor is the heroic poet bound by the "bare representation of what is true, or exceedingly probable" (1:153). Gods and disembodied spirits are allowed in epic poetry, and therefore in the heroic play. At the same time,

Dryden defends using the sound of trumpets and the shouts of fighting armies on the stage because he feels they contribute to the verisimilitude of theatrical performances and help create the dramatic delusion necessary to make the audience accept the effects of a heroic play, "for, though our fancy will contribute to its own deceit, yet a writer ought to help its operation" (1:155). Dryden's heroic plays show a certain consistency with his theory of the heroic play. Otherwise, except for his Shakespearean adaptations, he exhibits in his plays no strict adherence to critical theory.[21] His standards, on the contrary, are modified by his experience of writing plays.

Dryden's ambiguity in regard to the term *nature* is reflected in his conception of verisimilitude and probability. At times, his idea of verisimilitude is the same as that of Hobbes, who in his Preface to Davenant's *Gondibert,* stated: "Beyond the actual works of Nature, a poet may now go, but beyond the conceived possibilities of Nature, never." At other times, Dryden is more conscious of the distinction between the world of fiction and the world of reality. He then realizes that the poet constructs his own special imitation, which must be accepted on its own terms provided it bears some resemblance to the actual world and illustrates a moral truth. The latter conception of the inner probability of art is much closer to Aristotle's principle. Dryden never admitted that the audience demands that a stage performance be as real as actual life; on the contrary, in contrast to the rationalistic neo-Aristotelians, he stressed the initial act of imagination necessary to accept the system of probabilities within the play.[22] Dryden's artistic instinct at times led him to rebel against the predominant rationalism that increasingly stressed judgment over fancy and fact over the wonderful.

---

21. George Stuart Collins, *Dryden's Dramatic Theory and Praxis* (Leipzig: Schmidt, 1892), pp. 68-69.
22. Francis Gallaway, *Reason, Rule, and Revolt in English Classicism* (New York: C. Scribner's Sons, 1940), p. 126.

The Grounds of Criticism in Tragedy (1679) more conserva-
tively states that the action of a tragedy need not necessarily be
historically true, but there must be "a likeness of truth, something that is more than barely possible; *probable* being that which
succeeds, or happens, oftener than it misses" (1:209). In the
same work, however, Dryden commends the character of Cali-
ban, which seems to be outside nature, and he analyzes the process of imaginative synthesis by which Shakespeare created
such a character. The test of probability eventually becomes for
Dryden a matter of whether or not the play as a whole gives
pleasure to the audience. In fact, an argument could be made that
Dryden emancipated himself from criticism based on the imitation of nature.[23] Since the course of his criticism reveals continu-
ous ambivalence in the interpretation of the terms *nature* and
probability or verisimilitude, neat categories of critical standards
cannot be established for Dryden.

Dryden's serious consideration of Rymer's views is reflected
in the notes he compiled in 1677 or the next year on the end pages
of his copy of Rymer's *The Tragedies of the Last Age*.
Commenting favorably on the learned quality of Rymer's work
and recommending study of it, Dryden in his *Heads of an Answer
to Rymer* acknowledges that the design and execution of Greek
plays offer greater inducement to arousing pity and fear than
those of modern tragedy, but he will not concede that these excellences place the Greeks above the English dramatists. The Greeks
may excel in plot construction, but in expression, variety of
characters, and depiction of manners, the English are superior.
Dryden defends the English dramatic tradition and argues that
Rymer's case, based as it is upon attention to petty faults, remains unproved.

Dryden's reply to Rymer centers about the importance of the
fable or plot and the kind of emotions to be aroused by tragedy.

---

23. *Ibid.*, p. 129.

He does not agree with Rymer that plot is the soul of tragedy; it is only the foundation. A well-contrived plot will fail if the characters, manners, thought, and expression are unsuitable. He believes that there are other ends appropriate to tragedy besides that of arousing pity and fear. Stating that the English dramatists have fulfilled the moral purpose of drama as well as or better than the ancients, he asks—if tragedy must lead to the reformation of manners—are not all passions to be excited?

Dryden intends, through an examination of Aristotle's definition of tragedy, to find what his own position is in relation to the quarrel between the ancients and moderns. He questions that Aristotle could have said the final word on tragedy or on the tragic hero when he was familiar only with the plays of Sophocles, Euripides, and other Greek writers. Dryden conjectures, as he had previously in reference to the French, that Greek tragedy was relatively easy to write in comparison to the English, a form that has introduced larger plots and new passions, notably the noble passion of love. Saying that Shakespeare and Fletcher wrote for their own age, Dryden suggests that the means they employed are perhaps not inferior to those of the Greeks. He proposes to weigh the merits of English drama with those of the ancients, pointing out that the plays attacked by Rymer have evoked a favorable response from audiences—a response not attributable to the actors' skill, as Rymer had claimed.

Heads of an Answer to Rymer shows that, impressed as Dryden may have been by Rymer's case for the ancients in *The Tragedies of the Last Age,* he was not convinced about the superiority of Greek tragedy or about Aristotle's having established for all time an acceptable theory of tragedy. Dryden was concerned with a more flexible theory, which would place more emphasis on the standards of pleasure and audience response. He could not accept Rymer's critical straitjacket.

In the Preface to *All for Love* (1678) Dryden again opposes the rigidity of Rymer and attacks merely rationalistic criticism. Referring to Rymer's establishment of the ancients as models, he begins by calling attention to the excellent moral of *All for Love,* showing "famous patterns of unlawful love" with an appropriately unfortunate end (1:191). He notes too that the tragic hero should not be perfect or entirely wicked and that preferably his misdeeds should be involuntary, although this is regrettably not the case with Antony and Cleopatra. Pointing out that the tragic unities have been observed in *All for Love* more strictly than the English theater requires and that every scene contributes to the main design, and every act concludes "with a turn of it," Dryden replies to critics who have called attention to minor flaws in his work by saying that over-exact decorum makes a tragedy insipid (1:192). The French err in this respect. Lacking the genius of the British, they shine in trifles, but are often inept in essentials. He has endeavored in the play, he says, to follow the ancients, but the Greek models "are too little for English tragedy; which requires to be built in a larger compass" (1:200). Because he has attempted to imitate Shakespeare, he has dispensed with rhyme, although he has not abandoned his former view of it. Supporting genius over form in this preface, Dryden moves away from heroic drama and suggests that the rules should not be established deductively but reached inductively.

The Preface to *Troilus and Cressida* (1679) states Dryden's plan to explain the grounds of criticism in tragedy, taking as guides Aristotle and his interpreters, Horace and Longinus. *The Grounds of Criticism in Tragedy,* which follows, develops the ideas first suggested in *Heads of an Answer to Rymer.* Dryden reevaluates drama by Rymer's standards, finding much to object to and much to commend. He grants in detail, for example, the inadequacies of Shakespeare and Fletcher in respect to plotting, and then proceeds to discuss tragedy in terms of plot, character, manners, thought, and expression—following Le Bossu's method for the epic. He concentrates on plot and character —particularly on manners. He did not complete his intended

discussion of thought and expression. A less rigid follower of
Aristotelian tradition than Rymer, Dryden admired the *Poetics*,
but was more influenced by Horace, whose ideas he knew
firsthand, in contrast to those of Aristotle and Longinus, which
he became acquainted with through the French.[24]

Following a paraphrase of Aristotle's definition of tragedy,
Dryden states that the action in tragedy must be single because
two actions in tragedy detract from the involvement or "concernment" of the audience and thus nullify the purpose of the
poet—to move terror and pity. Furthermore, says Dryden, following Aristotle, the action should have a beginning, a middle,
and an end, and the persons represented, as well as the action,
should be great. Although the action should be probable, it does
not necessarily have to be historically true, but it must be plausible; it is to be represented and not told, to distinguish tragedy
from the epic. The end of tragedy, says Dryden, is "to rectify or
purge our passions, fear and pity" (1:209).

Dryden states that the general end of poetry is "to instruct de-
lightfully," whereas philosophy teaches by precept, a method
that is not so pleasurable (1:209). "To purge the passions by example, is therefore the particular instruction which belongs to
Tragedy" (1:209-10). Rapin has observed from Aristotle, notes
Dryden, "that pride and want of commiseration are the most predominant vices in mankind; therefore, to cure us of these two, the
inventors of Tragedy have chosen to work upon two other passions, which are fear and pity" (1:210). Fear is aroused by an example of terrible misfortune befalling "persons of the highest
quality" (1:210). We are thereby made conscious that no one is
spared the shifts of fortune. Terror is consequently stirred and
pride abated. "But when we see that the most virtuous, as well as
the greatest, are not exempt from such misfortunes, that consid-

---

24.   See Amanda M. Ellis, "Horace's Influence on Dryden," *PQ* 4 (1925): 39-60.

eration moves pity in us, and insensibly works us to be helpful to, and tender over, the distressed'' (1:210).

Dryden's comments on tragedy usually reflect a mixture of affective and fabulist thought characteristic of the bulk of later seventeenth-century criticism. *The Grounds of Criticism in Tragedy* follows Rapin's partly affective theory, his *Heads of an Answer to Rymer* something closer to the fabulist approach. In *Heads of an Answer to Rymer,* he finds Rapin's explanation of tragic fear and pity sufficient, but he does not want to limit the effects of tragedy to these two emotions. He tries simultaneously to defend Shakespeare and to approve poetic justice. In considering the emotional effect of a drama employing poetic justice, he suggests that a close examination is apt to show that the delight furnished by the stimulation of pity and fear in witnessing a tragedy is more important than the reward of the virtuous and the punishment of the wicked.[25] Generally, Dryden interprets the process of catharsis as ''evocative rather than purgative.''[26] Although the ends of tragedy are presented as social, these ends are to be achieved by psychological means. The fable does not so much demonstrate the workings of Providence as it provides a means of awakening ethical feeling. Dryden thought that the effects of moral utility and sweet embellishment depended on emotional response. A combination of the views of Aristotle and of Horace is the result.[27]

Rapin's theory, according to Hathaway, corresponds to the sentimental view of the eighteenth century. Loosely in the tradition of the Dutch scholar Heinsius, Rapin believed that tragedy should moderate excessive emotionality. It should arouse virtuous emotional response in those who lack feeling for others, but it

25.   Baxter Hathaway, ''John Dryden and the Function of Tragedy,'' *PMLA* 58 (September 1943):671.
26.   Eric Rothstein, ''English Tragedy in the Late Seventeenth Century,'' *ELH* 29 (September 1962):316.
27.   *Ibid.,* pp. 316-17.

should repress inappropriate sympathy for those who justly deserve their fate, and discourage excessive fear of the common sufferings of mankind. Heinsius's treatment of Aristotle's concept of catharsis differs from Dryden's only in emphasizing the necessity of repressing the excesses of emotionality. Dryden stresses the purgation. Rapin is midway between. Tragedy, Dryden said, develops our sense of pity and fear, both of which effects are good.[28]

In *An Essay of Dramatic Poesy* and in *A Defence of An Essay of Dramatic Poesy,* Dryden showed some tendency toward eighteenth-century sentimentalism. *An Essay of Dramatic Poesy* makes the purpose of a play to delight and to teach, and expresses respect for the principle of poetic justice. A tragic poet, Dryden also says, must be able to "stir up a pleasing admiration and concernment, which are the objects of a tragedy, and to show the various movements of a soul combating betwixt two different passions" (1:53). Aristotle's reference to fear, implying fear not for oneself but for the tragic hero, is changed to "concernment," and pity to admiration. *A Defence of An Essay of Dramatic Poesy* speaks of delight as the chief end of poetry, and states that the poet must "affect the soul, and excite the passions, and, above all . . . move admiration (which is the delight of serious plays)" (1:113).[29] The Preface to *An Evening's Love or the Mock Astrologer* (1671) refers to the instruction to be gained from tragedy and indicates that the Greek poets had generally adhered to poetic justice. The Preface to *All for Love* (1678) places more stress on pity. Pity is ascribed no moral function, but it replaces admiration as the chief emotional effect of tragedy.

Views that insist on poetic justice or on the function of tragedy to teach by example conflict with Dryden's modified concept of catharsis adapted from Rapin, because obviously the tragedies

28. Hathaway, *PMLA* 58 (September 1943): 667-68.
29. See J.E. Gillet, "A Note on the Tragic 'Admiratic,' " *MLR* 13 (1918): 233-38.

arousing the greatest pity are those in which predominantly virtuous characters suffer. Many times, Dryden assented to the doctrine of poetic justice, and, toward the end of his life, he explicitly employed the theories of Le Bossu, who made the function of art the teaching of morality.[30] Dryden's criticism reveals tension between his recognition of the freer vision of life made possible in poetry and the prevailing tendency to restrain such insight within the bounds of conventional morality. This conflict parallels Dryden's impulse toward poetic freedom warring with his respect for the rules.

In *The Grounds of Criticism in Tragedy,* Dryden considers the problem of how far Fletcher and Shakespeare are to be imitated in their plots, posing again the question he had previously introduced in *Heads of an Answer to Rymer.* They are to be imitated only insofar as they have copied those "who invented" and perfected dramatic poetry—allowing for superficial changes in religion, customs, and idioms of the language. Dryden's answer to how far Rymer's standards and those of the French formalists are to be followed is a compromise. He does, however, disagree with Rymer's judgment of *A King and No King,* a play that, he notes, illustrates the inferior sort of tragedy that ends happily. Dryden believes that the effectiveness of the play lies in the excellent touches of passion. In imperfect plots, he maintains, there are perhaps "less degrees of Nature" that arouse some measure of pity and fear in us. Dryden grasps the method of Beaumont and Fletcher's play—a decorative elaboration of emotion—and is responsive to it, as Rymer was not.[31]

Shakespeare, says Dryden, generally moves more terror, Fletcher, more compassion, "for the first had a more masculine, a bolder and more fiery genius; the second, a more soft and womanish" (1:212). In "the mechanic beauties of the plot"—the

30. Hathaway, *PMLA* 58 (September 1943): 670-71.
31. Arthur Mizener, "The High Design of *A King and No King,*" *MP* 38 (1940): 153.

unities of time, place, and action—both are deficient. Again
Dryden states, as he did in *Heads of an Answer to Rymer,* that
although the plot is the "groundwork" of tragedy, it frequently
does not make such an immediate impression as the excellences
or deficiencies of "the manners, the thoughts, and the expressions" (1:213).

Dryden applies to tragedy Le Bossu's principle that the writer
of epic must first establish a moral for his work. What is the
moral precept that the poet wishes to "insinuate into the people,"
Dryden asks (1:213). The moral directs the action of the play to
one center, "and that action or fable is the example built upon the
moral, which confirms the truth of it to our experience: when the
fable is designed, then, and not before, the persons are to be
introduced, with their manners, characters, and passions"
(1:213). Manners are the inclinations, "natural or acquired,"
that impel actions. They arise from humors, differences of age,
sex, climate, social status, or present conditions of the persons.
They may also be derived by the poet from knowledge of the
virtues, vices, and passions as described in philosophy, ethics,
and history—"of all which, whosoever is ignorant, does not
deserve the name of poet" (1:214).

Manners must be *apparent* [demonstrated in action and
discourse], *suitable* [appropriate to age, sex, and social status],
constant or *equal* [consistent], and have *resemblance* [be in accord with the historical or fictional reputation of a character].
Characters should be distinguished from one another by one ruling passion, Dryden believes—by which he does not mean one
virtue or vice, but "a composition of qualities which are not
contrary to one another in the same person; thus, the same man
may be liberal and valiant, but not liberal and covetous" (1:215).
Pity and terror, according to Dryden, must be principally founded
in the central character.

The Grounds of Criticism in Tragedy shows the influence of

Aristotle, Rapin, Le Bossu, and Rymer. Dryden agrees with Rymer in upholding poetic justice and in regarding the unities as "mechanic beauties," but he disagrees with his evaluation of Shakespeare and with his judgment that the Greeks are superior to the English in tragedy. *The Grounds of Criticism in Tragedy* reflects a more conventionally Aristotelian view of tragedy than any other work of Dryden. His theory of tragedy changes and fluctuates throughout his criticism because he was trying to reconcile two incompatible designs—the neoclassical and the Elizabethan.

Dryden's conception of the tragic hero as noble, though flawed, on the whole is Aristotelian. He departs from Aristotle in making the representation of character, manner, thought, and expression of equal importance with the plot. In dispensing with the chorus as unsuited to the English theater, he shows a better understanding of Aristotle than Rymer did. However, more directly than Aristotle, Dryden ascribes a social purpose to tragedy—to reform manners—a purpose that is achieved by the psychological process of catharsis. In general, Dryden's remarks on tragedy show a recurrently ambiguous conception of imitation as well as a repeated search for a new tragic theory, perhaps different from Aristotle's, that would be appropriate for his own age. In this respect, he was one of the moderns who believed in progress.

Dryden was a practicing poet, playwright, and critic who achieved distinction as all three. By means of open-minded discussion he analyzes the nature of poetry and tragedy to ascertain and to establish the essential technique, form, and psychological tone by which to express appropriately the peculiar genius of his age.

He is aware of the simplicity, clarity, and grandeur of Greek tragedy. He is also sensitive to the polish and precision of the French. By reason of both artistic insight and national feeling, however, he is attached to the breadth of imagination, the vitality, and variety of Elizabethan drama, particularly of Shakespeare's plays.

He begins with the belief that the true critic is not only responsive to a work of literature but capable of presenting his judgments analytically and of supporting them with discernibly reasonable clarification and evidence. His *examen* of Jonson's *The Silent Woman* is a special example of his method.

A true critic, he believes, understands at least the probable principles of the art with which he is concerned. He is further able to demonstrate these principles by showing how they emerge from specific works that he examines. The fact that his criticism relating to tragedy usually springs from consideration of existing plays, his own or those of the major Elizabethan dramatists, makes it predominantly inductive in approach.

Dryden assumes that the dramatist knows what he is doing and why, that he is a conscious craftsman, although especially endowed with "a happy genius." Dryden is scientific in his explanation of how certain effects in poetry and tragedy are achieved. His ratiocinative method, nevertheless, is imbued with sympathy, imagination, and vision. He holds his principles as a good scientist does, tentatively, at the same time examining contrary arguments. As with all flexible thinkers, therefore, he experiences periods when he tends to organize, clarify, even oversimplify the solutions to critical problems. Examples of this tendency may be seen in his excessive preoccupation with the unities and with dramatic "delusion" and in his almost compulsive defense of rhyme. Then again, reacting to the limitations of these views, particularly when chastened by experience with his own writing, he argues for greater freedom of poetic expression, and supports the larger scope of English drama in comparison with that of the Greek or the French.

He moved from an early metaphysical view of poetry to a

belief that poetry must demonstrate reasoned argument. Under the influence of Longinus, it is true, he veers for a time toward boldness of expression, if controlled by judgment, Primarily, his conception of poetry, although demonstrating a keen awareness of the importance of imagination, rests on Horace's *inventio* and on the conventional rhetorical divisions of *dispositio* and *elocutio*.[32] Imagination is the source of invention, fancy supplies the variation, and judgment insures propriety or accuracy in expression.

Throughout his criticism, Dryden is concerned with the problem of dramatic unity. All parts of a play must be necessary and must contribute to the total effect. *An Essay of Dramatic Poesy* stresses unity through variety. Later, in *A Parallel of Poetry and Painting*, Dryden thinks of dramatic unity in terms of perspective in painting, and in *The Grounds of Criticism in Tragedy* in terms of Aristotle's beginning, middle, and end. Never does he consider unity in tragedy a mere matter of presenting the events in the life of a central hero.

As do most critics of his age, he comes to favor circumscribing fancy by judgment. This is one basis of his defense of rhyme. It is also fundamental in his preoccupation with the unities. In this respect, he was a man of his time. He realized, no doubt, that the drama of the Elizabethans no longer suited the audience to which he wished to appeal. What he hoped to achieve, but perhaps never did, was a natural, proportionate, uncluttered work, having emotional force and intensity—the best qualities of classical literature—with, at the same time, some of the "variety and greatness of characters" in Shakespeare's plays. Above all, he wished to capture and retain some of the apparently effortless largeness of Shakespeare's imagination. Such a combination,

---

32. Lillian Feder, "John Dryden's Use of Classical Rhetoric," *Essential Articles for the Study of John Dryden*," ed. H. T. Swedenberg, Jr. (Hamden, Conn: Archon Books, 1966), pp. 493-518.

perhaps impossible at any time, certainly defied realization in an age of rationalism.[33]

In what opinions was Dryden steadily consistent? He believed in form, structure, and style. His historical sense led him to realize that it was impossible and undesirable to resurrect *in toto* either Greek drama or that of the Elizabethans, although he appreciated both. The French style he considered unsuited to the English temperament. It was too rigid, too narrow, too consciously flawless. These views, on the whole, are constant in his criticism, as is his devotion to Shakespeare's genius. In general, too, he recognizes the centrality of imagination in poetic creativity, preferring as he did Shakespeare to Jonson, although his detailed concern with technique frequently obscures this fact, particularly because of the later seventeenth-century association of imagination with uncontrolled or unnatural imagery. He tends, it is true, to be skeptical of the audience's capacity to exercise imagination. He was again in this respect aware of the temperament of his age.[34] In accordance, too, with the spirit of the time, his conviction that the language and conversation of his own day marked an advance over the ignorance of the Elizabethans is never repudiated.

Another constant element in Dryden's criticism is his conviction that poetry must be didactic. Sometimes he emancipates himself from this restraint to emphasize pleasure, but his preference for the epic and his attachment to Le Bossu attest to a steady conviction in regard to the social function of poetry and drama. He is somewhat consistent, too, in his preference for the imitation of nature as the ideal—at least in his own work. In this respect he is again a man of his time, although his appreciation of

---

33. See Ruth Wallerstein, "Dryden and the Analysis of Shakespeare's Techniques," *Essential Articles for the Study of John Dryden,* ed. H. T. Swedenberg, Jr. (Hamden, Conn.: Archon Books, 1966) pp. 551-75.
34. See Donald F. Bond, "Distrust of the Imagination in English Neo-Classicism." *PQ* 14 (January 1935): 54-69.

Shakespeare reflects intellectual tension in regard to the question. In *A Parallel of Poetry and Painting* he condemns tragicomedy as "wholly Gothic," but in general he supports it as psychologically sound. He consistently upholds the principle of probability, but his view—allowing for beings "out of nature"—is unrestrictive in comparison to Rymer's. Decorum, he insists, must be observed, but again not at the expense of a *"lively image of human nature."* Propriety of style, however, is always important to Dryden. Expression, he believes, should be natural, unexaggerated, and suited to the subject. He never wavers in his stress on poetry as a conscious art, for which the rules are an essential support. Dryden, from the beginning to the end, also points to one of the central difficulties in drama: to portray convincingly the emotional and psychological processes of character.

Aware of the effect on public taste of the Senecan tradition reflected in Shakespeare's drama, Dryden asks whether decorum requires complete exclusion of violence on the stage. What is propriety of expression? This is another question that he raises. How should characters in drama speak—in declamatory style or in short speeches? Related to his consideration of decorum and propriety is the very important realization that art works by means of convention. Choice of convention on the part of the dramatist depends to some extent on what the audience is prepared to accept. Hence, is rhyme or blank verse more effective?

In what ways do Dryden's opinions undergo change? Despite his didactic bent, he modifies his view of poetic justice as his conception of catharsis deepens. His support of the heroic play finally gives way to an attempt to adapt Shakespeare's drama to his own age. His preoccupation with plot is similarly modified by attention to manners, thought, and expression. His attitude toward the three unities is never quite clear or steady. He finally turns from the use of rhyme to the use of blank verse.

Beneath the intellectual gymnastics and changes of emphasis inevitable in Dryden's Socratic method lies a conservative steadiness of viewpoint. No drastic conversion to new theories or styles takes place. His method emerges as a reasonable means of justifying what he thinks is right. Dryden is a master stylist in prose, a critic who disciplines his intuitive response by judgment grounded in practicality. He is "the patron of all men of letters and of the poet turned critic."[35]

Dryden's criticism abounds in questions. A basic one is raised as a result of the ambiguity with which the term *nature* was used in the late seventeenth century. Nature had become too complex to define. Does imitating nature mean the imitation of actual life, of the typical, of the Platonic or social ideal, of *"la belle nature"*? Does it mean following the rules? Literal verisimilitude? Dramatic delusion? Or "a thing so almost infinite and boundless, as can never fully be comprehended, but where the images of all things are always present"? Dryden's criticism reflects the general confusion in regard to the meaning of the phrase *imitation of nature*.

Another term that resists clarification is *probability*. Does it mean the depiction of what is larger than life, what is confined within "the conceived possibilities of Nature," or is probability unlimited, resting only on a convincing basis for an initial exercise of the imagination on the part of the dramatist and his audience?

Imagination is a term also explored, if not clarified, by Dryden. Dryden is considered the first critic to use the term *imagination* in the sense of the faculty of the mind that gives rise to invention. He believed that, as the source of poetic invention, the imagination must work in harmony with judgment.

Other questions suggested by Dryden might be these: To what extent is tragedy related to the epic? Is Aristotle's definition of tragedy the final one? Does following the rules insure a positive audience response? Of what significance in critical evaluation is

---

35.   Helen Gardner, *The Business of Criticism* (Oxford: Clarendon Press, 1959), p. 27.

the effect of a play on the audience, even if the work does not correspond strictly to theoretical standards? For example, on the basis of effect, Dryden disputes Rymer's attack on Beaumont and Fletcher's *A King and No King*. The effect of the play, he claims, results from the excellent touches of passion that it displays. Jonson, he acknowledges, is the more correct poet, but Shakespeare arouses a stronger response in the audience. Dryden's consideration of the unities also reflects his attention to effect.

Dryden, T. S. Eliot said, "found the English speechless, and he gave them speech."[36] Dryden's two major contributions as a critic are of equivalent importance. First, he applied his ratiocinative method of analysis specifically to the works of Beaumont and Fletcher, Jonson and Shakespeare, and to his own. Not only were Dryden's judgments remarkably sound, but they were carefully reasoned and illustrated. Furthermore, and, no less important, he said what he wanted to say in a natural, conversational, yet precise way. The ease of Dryden's prose strikes the reader especially forcefully after the vitriolic extravagance of Rymer's and the weighty logic of Dennis's. One appreciates with fresh intensity the fact that Dryden is a stylist clever enough to erase any traces of conscious effort from his expression. Dryden had something to say, and he knew how to say it. His Socratic method, embracing as it does many viewpoints and contrary arguments, leaves the reader satisfied that Dryden's judgments are convincing—even after three centuries. His carefully reasoned analyses give the reader not only something to think about but a method for organizing his thinking. On the whole, Dryden wields the torch in criticism. If on occasion he takes the scepter in hand, he uses it as a tool for reasonable clarification and precise justification of his negative comments.

Dryden ascribed Shakespeare's defects to the deficiencies of his age. From the vantage point of the twentieth century, the

---

36. *John Dryden: The Poet, the Dramatist, the Critic*, p. 24.

same view may also be taken of Dryden's limitations as a critic.
In the perspective of time, this century may see the Elizabethans
as in some ways more discerning than the men of post-
Restoration England. Dryden was inclined to equate conscious
reasoning, clarity, and refinement with advancement in literature. It is our own age that has reversed this direction of thought,
emphasizing anew complexity, indefiniteness, and absurdity as
qualities of literary structure. As were other critics of his time,
Dryden was entangled with, but by no means strangulated by,
neo-Aristotelian theory. The arguments for the rules, it must be
admitted, still have a degree of validity. Dryden in this respect
expressed the genius of his age, as he wished to do.

Conclusion

What is particularly interesting for our time in the tragic theories of Rymer, Dennis, and Dryden? First, Rymer gives us a clear starting point for thinking about critical theory. By the very fact that he ignores many viewpoints that must be given consideration, he stimulates objections in our minds. He serves a useful function by offering us something firm against which to rebel.

In contrast, Dennis's Longinian standard of genius and the consequent recognition of art as process—as a creation in which mind and heart are one—strike a particularly contemporary note. His insistence upon a union of passion and vigorous thought based upon wide reading and broad experience of life represents what is best in the humanistic tradition. The absence of any unifying myth has been blamed for the mass anxiety of the twentieth century. What Dennis has to say about the relation of religion to tragedy therefore gives us something to consider.

Dryden's game of ideas, handled with wit and grace, offers a compromise between rigid authoritarianism on the one hand and critical anarchy on the other. He recognizes that critical standards must be reasonably supported and that a method of intelligent debate may lead to a civilized evolution in which both the value of tradition and the necessity for change are given full recognition. The critical works of Rymer, Dennis, and Dryden constitute important steps in the evolution of critical approaches to tragic theory.

Bibliography

List of Works Consulted

Abrams, M. H. *The Mirror and the Lamp: Romantic Theory and the Critical Tradition.* New York: Oxford University Press, 1953.

Aristotle. *Aristotle, On the Art of Poetry.* Translated by Ingram Bywater. Oxford: Clarendon Press, 1920.

_____. *The Basic Works of Aristotle.* Edited by Richard McKeon, New York: Random House, 1941.

Atkins, J. W. H. *English Literary Criticism: 17th and 18th Centuries.* London: Methuen, 1951.

_____. *Literary Criticism in Antiquity; A Sketch of its Development.* 2 vols. Gloucester, Mass.: P. Smith, 1961.

Bate, Walter Jackson. *From Classic to Romantic: Premises of Taste in Eighteenth-Century England.* Cambridge, Mass.: Harvard University Press, 1949.

Bohn, W. E. "The Development of John Dryden's Literary Criticism." *PMLA* 22, n. s. 15 (1907): 56-139.

Bond, Donald F. "Distrust of the Imagination in English Neo-Classicism." *PQ* 14 (January 1935): 54-69.

Bray, René. *La formation de la doctrine classique en France.* Paris: (n.p.), 1927.

Bredvold, Louis I. "Platonism in Neo-Classical Esthetics." *ELH* 1 (1934): 91-119.

130

_____. *The Intellectual Milieu of John Dryden.* Ann Arbor, Mich.: University of Michigan Press, 1934.

Buck, Philo M., Jr. *Literary Criticism; A Study of Values in Literature.* New York and London: Harper & Bros., 1930.

Butcher, S. H. *Aristotle's Theory of Poetry and Fine Art.* 4th ed. New York: Dover Publications, 1951.

Charlton, H. B. *Shakespearian Tragedy.* Cambridge: University Press, 1949.

Clark, Donald Lemen. *Rhetoric and Poetry in the Renaissance; A Study of Rhetorical Terms in English Renaissance Literary Criticism.* New York: Columbia University Press, 1922.

Collins, George Stuart. *Dryden's Dramatic Theory and Praxis.* Leipzig: Schmidt, 1892.

Cooper, Lane. *Aristotle On the Art of Poetry: An Amplified Version with Supplementary Illustrations.* rev. ed. Ithaca, N.Y.: Cornell University Press, 1947.

_____. *The Poetics of Aristotle: Its Meaning and Influence.* Boston: Marshall Jones Co., 1923.

Crane, R. S. "English Neoclassical Criticism." *Critics and Criticism.* Edited by R. S. Crane. Chicago: University of Chicago Press, 1952.

Daiches, David. *Critical Approaches to Literature.* Englewood Cliffs, N.J.: Prentice-Hall, Inc., 1956.

Dennis, John. *The Critical Works of John Dennis.* Edited by Edward Niles Hooker. 2 vols. Baltimore: Johns Hopkins Press, 1939, 1943.

Dollard, F. D. "French Influence on Thomas Rymer's Dramatic Criticism." Ph. D. diss., University of California, 1953.

Draper, John W. "Aristotelian 'Mimesis' in Eighteenth Century England." *PMLA* 36. (September 1921): 372-400.

Dryden, John. *Essays of John Dryden.* Edited by W. P. Ker. 2 vols. New York: Russell & Russell, 1961.

_____. *The Best of Dryden.* Edited by Louis I. Bredvold. New York: Ronald Press, 1933.

_____ *The Letters of John Dryden.* Edited by Charles E. Ward. Durham, N.C.: Duke University Press, 1942.

_____. *The Works of John Dryden.* Edited by Walter Scott and George Saintsbury. 18 vols. Edinburgh: W. Paterson, 1882-1893.

Dutton, G. B. "The French Formalists and Thomas Rymer." *PMLA* 29 (1914): 152-88.

Eliot, T. S. "A Dialogue of Poetic Drama," in *Of Dramatick Poesie, An Essay, 1668, by John Dryden;* preceded by *A. Dialogue on Poetic Drama, by T. S. Eliot*. London: F. Etchells & H. Macdonald, 1928.

_____. *John Dryden: The Poet, the Dramatist, the Critic*. New York: T. & Elsa Holliday, 1932.

_____. *Selected Essays, 1917-1932*. New York: Harcourt, Brace and Co., 1932.

Ellis, Amanda M. "Horace's Influence on Dryden." *PQ* 4 (1925): 39-60.

Else, Gerald F. *Aristotle's Poetics: The Argument*. Cambridge, Mass.: Harvard University Press. 1957.

_____. *The Origin and Early Form of Greek Tragedy*. Cambridge, Mass.: Published for Oberlin College by Harvard University Press, 1965.

Feder, Lillian. "John Dryden's Use of Classical Rhetoric," in *Essential Articles for the Study of John Dryden*. Edited by H. T. Swedenberg, Jr. Hamden, Conn.: Archon Books, 1966.

Friedland, L. S. "The Dramatic Unities in England." *Journal of English and Germanic Philology* 10: 56-89, 280-99, 453-67.

Frye, Northrop. *Anatomy of Criticism*. Princeton, N.J.: Princeton University Press, 1957.

Frye, P. H. "Dryden and the Critical Canons of the Eighteenth Century," in *Literary Reviews and Criticisms*. New York and London: G. P. Putnam's Sons, 1908.

Gallaway, Francis, *Reason, Rule, and Revolt in English Classicism*. New York: C. Scribner's Sons, 1940.

Gardner, Helen. *The Business of Criticism*. Oxford: Clarendon Press, 1959.

Garrett, Helen T. "The Imitation of the Ideal." *PMLA* 62 (September 1947): 735-44.

Gilbert, Allan, H. "The Aristotelian Catharsis." *The Philosophical Review* 35 (1926): 301-14.

Gillet, J. E. "A Note on the Tragic 'Admiratio.'" *MLR* 13 (1918): 233-38.

Green, C. C. *The Neo-classic Theory of Tragedy in England during the Eighteenth Century*. Cambridge, Mass.: Harvard University Press, 1934.

Hardison, O. B., Jr. *The Enduring Monument, A Study of the Idea of Praise in Renaissance Theory and Practice*. Chapel Hill, N.C.: University of North Carolina Press, 1962.

Hathaway, Baxter. *The Age of Criticism; the Late Renaissance in Italy*. Ithaca, N.Y.: Cornell University Press, 1962.

————. "John Dryden and the Function of Tragedy." *PMLA* 58 (September 1943): 665-73.

————. "The Lucretian 'Return upon Ourselves' in Eighteenth Century Theories of Tragedy." *PMLA* 62 (September 1947): 672-89.

Herrick, Marvin T. *The Fusion of Horatian and Aristotelian Literary Criticism, 1531-1555*. Illinois Studies in Language and Literature, vol. 32. Urbana, Ill.: University of Illinois Press, 1946.

————. *The Poetics of Aristotle in England*. New Haven, Conn.: Yale University Press, 1930.

Hobbes, Thomas. *Leviathan*. Edited and introduction by Michael Oakeshott. Oxford: Blackwell, 1960.

Horati, Flacci, Q. *Opera*, with previous annotations by Edward C. Wickham and current annotations by H. W. Garrod. London: Oxford University Press, 1963; first published 1901.

Johnson, Samuel. *Lives of the English Poets*. Introduction by Arthur Waugh. 2 vols. New York: Oxford University Press, 1906.

Krutch, Joseph Wood. *Comedy and Conscience After the Restoration*. New York: Columbia University Press, 1924.

Legouis, Pierre. "Corneille and Dryden as Dramatic Critics," *Seventeenth Century Studies Presented to Sir Herbert Grierson*. Oxford: Clarendon Press, 1938.

Literary Criticism, Plato to Dryden. Edited by Allan H. Gilbert. New York: American Book Co., 1940.

Longinus. *Longinus On the Sublime*. Edited by W. Rhys Roberts. 2nd ed. Cambridge: University Press, 1907.

Lovejoy, A. O. "'Nature' as Aesthetic Norm." *Essays in the History of Ideas*. Baltimore: Johns Hopkins Press, 1948.

————. "The Parallel of Deism and Classicism." *Essays in the History of Ideas*. Baltimore: Johns Hopkins Press, 1948.

Lucas, F. L. *Tragedy; Serious Drama in Relation to Aristotle's Poetics*. Rev. and enl. ed. London: Hogarth Press, 1957.

McKeon, Richard, "Literary Criticism and the Concept of Imitation in Antiquity," in *Critics and Criticism*. Edited by R. S. Crane. Chicago: University of Chicago Press, 1952.

Milton, John. *John Milton, Complete Poems and Major Prose.* Edited by Merritt Y. Hughes. New York: Odyssey Press, 1957.

Mizener, Arthur. "The High Design of *A King and No King.*" *MP* 38 (1940): 133-154.

Monk, Samuel Holt. "Dryden Studies: A Survey, 1920-45." *ELH* 14 (March 1947): 46-63.

―――. *John Dryden: A List of Critical Studies Published from 1895 to 1948.* 1st ed. Minneapolis, Minn.: University of Minnesota Press, 1950.

―――. *The Sublime; A Study of Critical Theories in XVIII-Century England.* New York: Modern Language Association of America, 1935; Ann Arbor, Mich.: University of Michigan Press, 1960.

Nicoll, Allardyce. *An Introduction to Dramatic Theory.* New York: Brentano, 1923.

Nicolson, Marjorie. "The Early Stages of Cartesianism in England." *Studies in Philology* 26: 355-74.

Osborn, James M. *John Dryden: Some Biographical Facts and Problems.* rev. ed. Gainesville, Fla.: University of Florida Press, 1965.

Paul, H. G. *John Dennis, His Life and Criticism.* New York: Columbia University Press, 1911.

Plato. *Laws.* 2 vols. (9, 10). Translated by R. G. Bury in *Plato, with an English Translation,* London: W. Heinemann; New York: G. P. Putnam's Sons, 1926.

―――. *The Republic of Plato.* Translated and with introduction and notes by Francis M. Cornford. New York: Oxford University Press, 1945.

Rapin, René. *Les Oeuvres.* 3 vols. Amsterdam: chez Pierre Mortier, 1695-1709.

Ridgeway, William. *The Origin of Tragedy with Special Reference to the Greek Tragedians.* Cambridge: University Press, 1910.

Rothstein, Eric. "English Tragic Theory in the Late Seventeenth Century." *ELH* 29 (September 1962): 306-23.

Russell, Trusten Wheeler. *Voltaire, Dryden & Heroic Tragedy.* New York: Columbia University Press, 1946.

Rymer, Thomas. *The Critical Works of Thomas Rymer.* Edited with introduction and notes by Curt A. Zimansky. New Haven, Conn.: Yale University Press, 1956.

Saintsbury, George. *A History of Criticism and Literary Taste in*

Europe. 2nd ed. 3 vols. Edinburgh and London: William Blackwood and Sons, 1911.

_____. *Dryden.* London and New York: Harper & Bros., 1930.

Sharp, Robert Lathrop. *From Donne to Dryden.* Chapel Hill, N.C.: University of North Carolina Press, 1940.

Sherwood, Margaret. *Dryden's Dramatic Theory and Practice.* Boston, New York, London: Lamson, Wolffe and Co., 1898.

Shumaker, Wayne. *Perspectives in Criticism.* Berkeley, Calif.: University of California Press, 1952.

Sidney, Sir Philip. *A Defence of Poetry.* Edited by J. A. Van Dorsten. London: Oxford University Press, 1966.

Sikes, E. E. *The Greek View of Poetry.* London: Methuen, 1931.

Smith, David Nichol. *John Dryden.* Cambridge: University Press, 1950.

Smith, John H. "Dryden's Critical Temper." *Washington University Studies, Humanistic Series* 2 (April 1925): 201-20.

Spingarn, J. E. *Critical Essays of the Seventeenth Century,* 1908 ed. 3 vols. Bloomington, Ind.: Indiana University Press, 1963.

Thorndike, Ashley H. *Tragedy.* Boston and New York: Houghton, Mifflin Co., 1908.

Thorpe, Clarence D. *The Aesthetic Theory of Thomas Hobbes.* Ann Arbor, Mich.: University of Michigan Press, 1940, and New York: Russell & Russell, 1964.

Trowbridge, Hoyt. "Dryden's *Essay on the Dramatic Poetry of the Last Age.*" *PQ* 22 (July 1943): 240-50.

_____. "The Place of Rules in Dryden's Criticism." *MP* 44 (November 1946): 84-96.

Van Doren, Mark. *John Dryden, A Study of His Poetry.* 3rd ed. New York: H. Holt and Co., 1946.

Verrall, A. W. *Lectures on Dryden.* Cambridge: University Press, 1914.

Walcott, F. G. "John Dryden's Answer to Thomas Rymer's *The Tragedies of the Last Age.*" *PQ* 15 (April 1936): 194-214.

Wallerstein, Ruth. "Dryden and the Analysis of Shakespeare's Techniques." *Essential Articles for the Study of John Dryden.* Edited by H. T. Swedenberg, Jr. Hamden, Conn: Archon Books, 1966.

Ward, Charles E. *The Life of John Dryden.* Chapel Hill, N.C.: University of North Carolina Press, 1961.

Wasserman, Earl. "The Pleasures of Tragedy." *ELH* 14 (1947): 283-307.

Weinberg, Bernard A. *A History of Literary Criticism in the Italian Renaissance.* 2 vols. Chicago: University of Chicago Press, 1961.

_____. "Castelvetro's Theory of Poetics," in *Critics and Criticism.* Edited by R. S. Crane. Chicago: University of Chicago Press, 1952.

_____. "Scaliger versus Aristotle on Poetics." *MP* 39 (May 1942); 337-60.

Wellek, René. *The Rise of English Literary History.* Chapel Hill, N.C.: University of North Carolina Press, 1941.

_____ and Warren, Austin. *Theory of Literature.* New York: Harcourt, Brace and Co., 1949.

Willey, Basil. *The Seventeenth Century Background.* London: Chatto & Windus, 1942.

Williamson, George. "The Occasion of *An Essay of Dramatic Poesy.*" *MP* 44 (August 1946): 1-9.

Wimsatt, William K., Jr. "The Structure of the 'Concrete Universal' in Literature." *PMLA* 62 (March 1947): 262-80.

_____ and Brooks, Cleanth. *Literary Criticism; A Short History.* New York: Knopf, 1957.

Wood, P. S. "The Opposition to Neo-Classicism in England between 1660 and 1700." *PMLA* 43 (1928): 182-97.

Young, Kenneth, *John Dryden, A Critical Biography.* London: Sylvan Press, 1954.

Index

Abrams, M. H., 14

Action in tragedy, 14-17, 21, 56, 77, 80, 111, 113, 116, 120; Aristotle's meaning of, 14; Aristotle's unity of, 17-18, 29, 31-32. *See also* Fable; Plot

Addison, Joseph: *Cato*, 80-81

Admiration as a tragic emotion, 26, 29, 69, 118

Advancement and Reformation of Modern Poetry, The (Dennis), 62, 63, 64, 68, 74

Aeschylus, 39

Alazon, Othello as, 58

Alchemist, The (Jonson), 106

All for Love (Dryden), 77, 115

Anagnorisis, 21

Ancients and Moderns: Dennis and, 68, 87; Dryden and, 114, 121; Rymer and, 39

Apology for Poetry (Sidney). See *Defence of Poesie*

Aristotle, 13-32 passim, 42; aesthetic distance of, 73; Dennis and, 13, 32, 64, 67, 72-86 passim; Dryden and, 13, 32, 89, 91, 94, 97-100, 103, 112-26 passim; *Poetics*, 13-23, 27-32, 43, 45, 90, 116; *Politics*, 24; *Posterior Analytics*, 94; Renaissance critics and, 39-40;

Rhetoric, 22; Rymer and, 13, 32, 34-37 passim, 53-54, 58-59; tradition of, 39-40. *See also* Action in tragedy; Character; Critic; Decorum; Expression; Imitation; *Mimesis;* Plot; Poetry and history; Probability; Spectacle; Thought; Tragic hero

Ars poetica (Horace), 18, 43, 100

Art poëtique, L' (Boileau), 30

Audience response, 14, 18; Castelvetro on, 28; Dennis and, 61, 79; Dryden and, 36-37, 89, 91, 113, 114, 126-27; Rymer and, 34, 36, 40, 47-48, 50

Bale, John: *King John*, 72

Beaumont, Francis, and Fletcher, John, 40-41, 46, 104, 108, 119-20, 127; *King and No King, A*, 40, 119, 127; *Maid's Tragedy, The*, 40, 106; *Rollo*, 40. See *also* Fletcher

Bellori, Giovanni Pietro: *Lives of the Painters*, 110

Blank verse in tragedy: Dennis on, 71; Dryden on, 103-4, 125

Bohn, William E.: "The Development of John Dryden's Literary Criticism," 95-96